SUMMER MOVIES

30

**SUN-DRENCHED
CLASSICS**

TURNER **CLASSIC** MOVIES

30

**SUN-DRENCHED
CLASSICS**

JOHN MALAHY

FOREWORD BY LEONARD MALTIN

RUNNING PRESS
PHILADELPHIA

Running Press
Hachette Book Group
1290 Avenue of the Americas, New York, NY 10104
www.runningpress.com
@Running_Press

Printed in Thailand

First Edition: May 2021

Published by Running Press, an imprint of Perseus Books, LLC, a subsidiary of Hachette Book Group, Inc. The Running Press name and logo is a trademark of the Hachette Book Group.

The Hachette Speakers Bureau provides a wide range of authors for speaking events. To find out more, go to www.hachettespeakersbureau.com or call (866) 376-6591.

The publisher is not responsible for websites (or their content) that are not owned by the publisher.

All images courtesy of Turner Classic Movies.

Print book cover and interior design by Jenna McBride.

Library of Congress Control Number: 2020949830

ISBNs: 978-0-7624-9929-8 (hardcover), 978-0-7624-9927-4 (ebook)

RRD-S

10 9 8 7 6 5 4 3 2 1

CONTENTS

What kind of book devotes equal time to Ingmar Bergman and Frankie Avalon? Answer: the one you're reading right now.

That's because its author, John Malahy, has taken an admirably broad view of his subject, opening with the celebrated silent film *Lonesome* and closing with the equally illustrious Italian movie *Call Me by Your Name*. If you want to find a narrower, more predictable survey of so-called summer movies, feel free to browse online. This book was clearly compiled by an aficionado who's knowledgeable enough to be familiar with the silent era, the golden age of Hollywood, foreign-language films, and contemporary cinema. He is happily devoid of snobbery and pretension.

As a bona fide baby boomer and self-styled "indoor" kid, summer meant one thing above all else to me: the freedom to go to the movies any day of the week I chose. That meant that I got to see *The Parent Trap* (starring Hayley Mills and Hayley Mills) the first week it played in a nearby New Jersey theater. Yet I don't remember classifying anything I saw as a "summer movie." There were just films I happened to see when school was out of session.

One summer, the Fox Theatre in Hackensack (long gone) set up a Tuesday matinee series and issued an oversized ticket with twelve numbers on the edge. Every week a theater employee would punch a hole in the proper space to show that I'd attended and watched a chapter of the old Columbia serial *The Great Adventures of Wild Bill Hickok*. Since it consisted of fifteen chapters and we had only twelve weeks to watch them all, the theater gave us double doses several times, which in theory was okay but in reality exposed all the ways the serial cheated on its cliffhanger chapter endings. I guess you could say I got a bit more movie-savvy that summer. I also got in for free the final week because I'd had perfect attendance.

Judy Garland and Gene Kelly rehearse in *Summer Stock* (1950).

Observers of popular culture agree that the term "summer movie" came into play with the release of Steven Spielberg's blockbuster *Jaws* in 1975. It was among the first films I know of that inspired exhibitors to clear the auditorium after every showing. Word-of-mouth reaction to the film was so strong that people went back to see it again and again, mushrooming its box-office receipts. I had been married only three months when the picture was released, and my wife Alice's elbow was black and blue from my grabbing it at every "jump scare" that came along. The other thing we both recall is that people stayed out of the ocean that summer—and for several summers to follow.

I also remember the tension that preceded the release of Spike Lee's *Do the Right Thing*. It was so thick you could cut it with a knife . . . but for the most part, audiences absorbed this provocative drama without exploding into violence as some pundits had predicted. Many of the films Malahy documents in this book had a lasting impact on moviegoers. Decades after its release, women of all ages still relate to Jennifer Grey's "Baby" in *Dirty*

Katharine Hepburn and Rossano Brazzi arrive on Burano in *Summertime* (1955).

Dancing, and the depiction of a typical American family in *National Lampoon's Vacation* continues to ring true, allowing for comic exaggeration.

Most of all, John Malahy captures the fun we associate with summertime, whether or not we take his suggestions for travel and tourism or line up some of his outside-the-box suggestions for double features. This book made me smile, remembering when and where I first encountered the films he discusses so enthusiastically. If you haven't seen all thirty features, you have even more to look forward to. Remember, a good movie is never out of season.

LEONARD MALTIN is best known for his evergreen reference paperback *Leonard Maltin's Movie Guide*, its offshoot *Leonard Maltin's Classic Movie Guide*, and his thirty-year run on Entertainment Tonight. He teaches at the USC School of Cinematic Arts and appears on Turner Classic Movies. With his daughter Jessie he hosts the weekly podcast *Maltin on Movies*. He also holds court at www.leonardmaltin.com.

INTRODUCTION

I n June 1975, Steven Spielberg's *Jaws* was released in theaters. The summer-set thriller kicked off an industry trend: the crucial season in which studios release their biggest movies while teenagers (the target audience) are home from school. But *Jaws* isn't just the prototypical summer blockbuster. It is also a classic example of an underappreciated category of movies—those that depict the experiences, traditions, and delights of the summer season. As such, Spielberg's monster movie can be linked to other warm-weather classics, from beach musicals to sun-drenched romances.

Much of our understanding of summer comes from, or is reflected in, the movies. The great American road trip will probably always be tied to the Griswolds and their iconic green station wagon. Gidget is the quintessential teenage misfit who, both literally and figuratively, finds her place in the sun. "There's no crying in baseball!" continues to be heard on many a warm afternoon at the ballpark. Better still, these cultural touchstones can be accessed any time of year. Even in the chilly depths of winter, the movies can bring us the feeling of a carefree summer's day.

This book sprang from my personal love of *Jaws* and quickly grew in scope to cover everything from Betty Grable to Patrick Swayze. At first, there was a century's worth of titles from which to select, spanning Charlie Chaplin's short *By the Sea* (1915)—a self-styled "classic of girls, the seashore and the good old summer time"—to *Spider-Man: Far from Home* (2019), in which the high school superhero takes a class trip to Venice.

But summer is more than just a time for R&R. The downside of all that warm weather is the threat of violent hurricanes and killer heat waves, as seen in *Key Largo* (1948) and *Rear Window* (1954). The swelter of a New York summer features in both Billy Wilder's frothy

Carole Landis and Robert Cummings in *Moon Over Miami* (1941)

Spike Lee as Mookie in *Do the Right Thing* (1989)

rom-com *The Seven Year Itch* (1955) and Spike Lee's searing portrait of inner-city life, *Do the Right Thing* (1989). Cinema is a universal medium, and filmmakers from France, Japan, Italy, Sweden, and virtually every other nation have put to celluloid their versions of summer—hence the presence of films by Jacques Tati and Ingmar Bergman.

Notably absent are movies that explicitly take place at other times of year—such as the college spring break romp *Where the Boys Are* (1960)—or ones that don't speak to the summer experience in any universal way, like the otherwise essential *Dog Day Afternoon* (1975). A popular film like *Grease* (1978) may imbue the summer with meaning ("Those summer nights!") but, except for a brief opening sequence, doesn't actually depict it.

In many films, summer offers an escape from the routine of everyday life, from the drudgery of work and the pressures of the school year. The movies often depict literal getaways: travel, adventure, and new ways of experiencing the world, as with Katharine Hepburn's globetrotting heroine in *Summertime* (1955). Warm weather also allows for a reentry into nature, and films like *Moonrise Kingdom* (2012) take place primarily in the wilderness, outside of the built environment. Beach movies like *Gidget* (1959) and *Beach Blanket Bingo* (1965) are set on the edge of civilization, where the sand and surf become a fertile space for counterculture. *The Endless Summer* (1964), which contains only one brief scene shot inside a building, draws all of its energy from the natural world.

Each year, the summer season presents itself as a blank slate, full of opportunity and time for new perspectives on our lives. The main characters in many of the best summer movies often go through a process of self-discovery. They find new hobbies, new interests, new ways of living. In *The Parent Trap* (1961), two teenagers literally discover who they are. New love is also in the air, with budding romances featured in everything from *Lonesome* (1928) to *Call Me by Your*

Tom Hanks and Geena Davis in *A League of Their Own* (1992)

Top: Timothée Chalamet and Armie Hammer swim in *Call Me by Your Name* (2017).
Bottom: The Griswolds take the road less traveled in *National Lampoon's Vacation* (1983).

Julie Delpy and Ethan Hawke wander Vienna in *Before Sunrise* (1995).

Name (2017). In some cases—*The Graduate* (1967) and *Breaking Away* (1979)—young people find themselves in a season of limbo between the end of one life and the start of another.

This book delivers a diversity of tone and genre, from musicals to noir and even a documentary. But one key area where movies historically come up short, and summertime films falter in particular, is diversity of voices. This is a problem that I cannot fully resolve in these pages, despite an entry here or there that represents an alternative experience. One bright spot, however, is the multitude of empowered women characters, from Jane in *Summer Stock* (1950) to Baby in *Dirty Dancing* (1987), who grace the screen with stories of determination and triumph.

Interestingly, though almost every decade of movie history is represented, some are much more prominent

than others. History shows us that summer fun ebbs and flows in the cinema, with economic booms (during the 1950s, for example) acting as catalysts, blessing peacetime America with more disposable income—which in turn leads to more summer-set films (1955 alone is represented by four movies). On the flip side, when the United States was in a dark moment, or when serious world events dominated the subject of film content, summer movies didn't really break through, as evidenced by a dearth of such films from the eras of the Great Depression, World War II, and the Vietnam War.

What follows is a subjective sampling of summer movies, not meant to be exhaustive or encyclopedic. I

Jacques Tati in *Monsieur Hulot's Holiday* (1953)

invite readers to dig further into the themes and genres that speak to them. To that end, I include a suggestion for a double feature with each main entry, along with a fun suggestion for a vacation or activity themed to the film.

Most importantly, I hope these movies bring you the joy of summer all year round and inspire you to create your own magic moments under the sun.

Mickey Rooney, Lewis Stone, and Cecilia Parker on vacation in *You're Only Young Once* (1937)

LONESOME

Two single New Yorkers share a romantic Fourth of July weekend at Coney Island.

Director Paul Fejos ● **Producer** Carl Laemmle Jr. ● **Story** Mann Page, scenario by Edward T. Lowe Jr., dialogue and titles by Tom Reed

Starring **Barbara Kent** Mary ● **Glenn Tryon** Jim ● **Andy Devine** Jim's Friend
Fay Holderness Overdressed Woman ● **Gustav Partos** Romantic Gentleman
Eddie Phillips The Sport

Universal, 1928
B&W
69 min.

Ever since the movies began, audiences have sought romance on the big screen. One highlight from the silent era is this summertime film about a pair of overworked city dwellers who take some much-needed R&R at Coney Island. They meet on the beach, form a connection, and spend the afternoon together. Unfortunately, they fail to exchange personal details, so when they become separated in the crowd after a roller-coaster accident, these star-crossed lovers have little chance of ever finding each other again. But have no fear—Hollywood has a happy ending in store.

The first sequence introduces the two main characters separately. Mary is played by Barbara Kent, the former Miss Hollywood of 1925, who was by that time a contract player with Universal. Neither she nor the actor playing Jim, Glenn Tryon, is particularly well known today, but their anonymity may actually strengthen the movie's universal appeal: these characters could be anyone. And like a lot of people, they're slaves to the alarm clock. Summer has arrived, but Mary and Jim are trapped in their routine. Because it's a Saturday (July 3, to be precise) they both work a half shift before being let out early for the holiday. While their coworkers pair off and make exciting plans, Jim and Mary are single and lonely, and a tad too self-conscious. After a bit of

Studio founder Carl Laemmle put his name on virtually every Universal film, but his son, Carl Laemmle Jr., was the supervising producer on *Lonesome*.

moping, each decides to make the most of the free time and takes off for Coney Island.

But if the city is crowded and impersonal, so is the shore. Filled with people, the beach doesn't appear to be very relaxing, but—as luck would have it—it's where Jim and Mary meet, have a conversation (literally, thanks to Movietone sound technology), and begin to

◄◄ **Opposite page:** Glenn Tryon tries out his luck, with Barbara Kent.

fall for each other. After taking in the evening lights of Coney Island and enjoying a few rides, they head to the dance hall, where the camera isolates the couple against a fanciful background. It's clear that everything else has faded from their minds.

Most audiences today have likely never heard of *Lonesome*, nor its director or stars. But the movie is a treasure, and it deserves to be in the same conversation as other early landmarks like F. W. Murnau's *Sunrise* (1927). These two films were produced at the same point in history: the years straddling the silent and sound eras, when cinema was simultaneously at its artistic zenith and in the throes of major technological change. In fact, *Lonesome* premiered as a fully silent film and a few months later was rereleased with a musical track, sound effects, and dialogue sequences. For instance, audiences can now hear Irving Berlin's popular tune "Always," which serves to unite—and later reunite—the lovers.

Thanks to a restoration by the George Eastman House, the virtuosic style of *Lonesome* is available today for all to see. The movie makes lavish use of superimpo-sition, along with optical printing effects aided by newly available film stocks. The camera moves fluidly to express character, emotion, and conflict, as when Jim performs a handstand and the camera mimics him by playfully turning itself upside down. The nighttime portion of the film features several striking colorized sequences of Coney Island rides and attractions. A climactic storm sequence, in which rain pours on the crowd and wind howls through the boardwalk, is especially impressive.

Universal was more than capable of filming *Lonesome* on location in New York, but the filmmakers chose instead to shoot entirely in California, including boardwalk sequences at Venice and Long Beach. Stock footage of Coney Island was then sprinkled liberally throughout. The goal wasn't verisimilitude, but an impressionistic rendering of the midway. Film professor Richard Koszarski dubs the result "a Coney Island of the mind." Instead of replicating the world in a realistic way, director Paul Fejos prioritizes the psychological experience of the characters, displaying their inner lives in visual terms.

Vacation Inspiration

Coney Island still delights millions every summer and is easily reachable by subway if you're in the New York area. Enjoy the current Luna Park, take a spin on the Wonder Wheel, stroll the boardwalk, and grab a hot dog at Nathan's Famous. Or just plant your umbrella on the beach—you never know who you might run into.

An easy getaway for millions of New Yorkers since the mid-nineteenth century, Coney Island is an icon of leisure. It was once christened "America's Playground" and has for decades represented both the ideal day at the beach and the classic amusement park. The 1920s were a particularly booming time for the resort. Its iconic Ferris wheel, the Wonder Wheel, opened in 1920, and the famous boardwalk connected the various parks in 1923. New roller coasters were added, including the original Thunderbolt (later famously depicted in 1977's *Annie Hall*) and the Coney Island Cyclone, which is still in operation. Many films of the era were shot on location there, including Paramount's *The King on Main Street* (1925) and Harold Lloyd's *Speedy* (1928). And it continues to feature in movies today, such as the coming-of-age drama *Beach Rats* (2017).

Paul Fejos was Hungarian and only worked in the United States for a brief period. He arrived in Los Angeles in 1926 and pulled together the financing to produce an independent, avant-garde film called *The Last Moment* (1928), made with cinematographer Leon Shamroy. That film, now considered lost, was impressive enough for producer Carl Laemmle Jr. to invite Fejos to Universal, where he completed *Lonesome* (which made money) and two other films (which did not) before becoming disenchanted with Hollywood. In the late 1930s he traveled the world as an ethnographic filmmaker, working in far-flung places like Madagascar and the Amazon River

Barbara Kent as Mary

basin. He later became director of research at the Viking Fund, an anthropological organization.

Fejos confessed that he found Hollywood to be "phony," an understandable reaction from someone who wished to show how everyday people lived and worked together in society. This ethos comes across in *Lonesome*, which shines a spotlight on two average individuals. Though mundane, their story matters just as much as any prestigious drama being made in Hollywood.

Lonesome is a movie about a summertime romance, but like many of the films in this book, the season is merely a conduit for other, deeper revelations. As its title would suggest, *Lonesome* is really about alienation in the modern world, and it uses the joys of summer to offer a hopeful solution.

Make It a Double Feature

Speedy (Paramount, 1928)

Harold Lloyd's romp through New York City includes a famous sequence shot in Coney Island, where he and his sweetheart Jane (Ann Christy) visit Luna and Steeplechase parks. Although the boardwalk scenes were filmed in California, as they were in *Lonesome*, many of the real attractions are shown, including Luna's Witching Waves and Shoot the Chutes, with cameras placed on several of the rides for extra effect. *Speedy* also features a notable cameo from Babe Ruth, whom Harold drives breathlessly to Yankee Stadium. The film is equal parts summertime fun and love letter to the Jazz Age city.

Ann Christy and Harold Lloyd

YOU'RE ONLY YOUNG ONCE

The Hardy family spends their summer vacation on Catalina Island, where young Andy learns the ins and outs of dating.

Director George B. Seitz ● **Producer** Carey Wilson ● **Screenplay** Kay Van Riper, based on characters by Aurania Rouverol

Starring **Lewis Stone** Judge Hardy ● **Mickey Rooney** Andy Hardy
Cecilia Parker Marian Hardy ● **Fay Holden** Mrs. Hardy ● **Ann Rutherford** Polly Benedict
Sara Haden Aunt Milly ● **Eleanor Lynn** Geraldine "Jerry" Lane ● **Ted Pearson** Bill Rand

MGM, 1937
B&W, 78 min.

T he Hardys are a stereotypical midwestern family, the paragon of middle-class America as imagined by Hollywood. Long before shows like *Father Knows Best* (1954–1960) and *Leave It to Beaver* (1957–1963) lit up television screens, Judge Hardy and his family entertained audiences with wholesome domestic drama. They quickly became some of MGM's most popular characters, and installments in the series were guaranteed moneymakers. Starting with *A Family Affair* (1937), the studio pumped out a total of fifteen Andy Hardy features within a decade.

But no knowledge of the others is needed to appreciate *You're Only Young Once*. The second film in the series, it stands on its own as a charming family vacation comedy that follows the Hardy clan on a trip to the West Coast.

When the film opens each family member has an idea of how to best spend their vacation—most of which involves spending time away from each other. Teenage Andy (Mickey Rooney) wants to follow his girlfriend, Polly (Ann Rutherford), to Pebble Cove. Older sister Marian (Cecilia Parker) pines for her boyfriend, but if her family were to visit the resort at Lake Beauty, she might be able to see him. Meanwhile, Mrs. Hardy (Fay Holden) suggests a cottage at Ocean Grove, to be near her relatives.

Third billed, Mickey Rooney had yet to become the star of the Hardy films.

⬅ **Opposite page: Eleanor Lynn makes an impression on Mickey Rooney.**

But Judge Hardy (Lewis Stone) has other ideas and surprises them with a trip to Santa Catalina Island. "What's a vacation for?" he asks. "It ought to give us all a chance to meet people that otherwise we'd never get to know. Talk to 'em, get new viewpoints. That's why I want to go so far away. The Hardy family needs new perspectives and Catalina will give 'em to us." Indeed it will, but the Judge also privately wants to do some

Andy Hardy (Mickey Rooney) tries to stay true to girlfriend Polly (Ann Rutherford).

swordfishing—a fact that becomes apparent when a new rod and reel arrive in the mail.

The film shifts to Catalina (depicted via some gorgeous location footage), where the family settles into a homey cottage a few blocks from the sea. The Judge soon gets more than he bargained for. Marian becomes attached to a married lifeguard, Bill (Ted Pearson), who explains that a divorce is imminent. Andy likewise falls hard for the first girl he meets: the worldly Jerry Lane (Eleanor Lynn), whose mother is currently in Reno getting a divorce of her own. Jerry represents an easy sexuality; unlike Polly, she lets Andy kiss her on their first date and the red-blooded young man is pretty much beside himself. The film begs us to ask: maybe going to California wasn't such a great idea?

Only an hour by boat from Long Beach, Catalina Island was used for location shooting by Hollywood for decades and often doubled for Polynesia, as it had recently done in MGM's epic *Mutiny on the Bounty* (1935). Even today its beaches, hiking trails, and laid-back vibe make it a great place for a weekend getaway.

The central concern of *You're Only Young Once* is whether Andy—naive and impulsive—can rise to maturity, or if he still needs guidance from his parents. The story follows a pattern that will recur throughout the series: Andy somehow gets into trouble, Judge Hardy confronts his own adult problems—here, a real estate loan gone afoul—and a final act man-to-man talk will allow the Judge to impart wisdom to his son.

The Hardy series had originally stemmed from dramatist Eugene O'Neill's 1933 play *Ah, Wilderness!*, a coming-of-age story set on the Fourth of July, which was made into a film at MGM in 1935. When it became a box-office success, its cast—which included Lionel Barrymore, Wallace Beery, and Spring Byington, along with Rooney and Parker—was assigned to *A Family Affair*, with a story centered around a similar domestic space. Based on the 1928 play *Skidding* by Aurania Rouverol, the first Andy Hardy film wasn't about Andy in particular, but Rooney's character soon broke out as the main draw for audiences, and his name would later be used regularly in the films' titles. The success of *A Family Affair* led studio chief Louis B. Mayer to design a series of sequels, each shot at a B-level budget, to be presented as the second billed movie in a double feature. The combination of low costs, efficient shooting (*You're Only Young Once* was completed in less than three weeks), and huge audience appeal made the Hardy series one of the biggest returns on investment in MGM's history. Mayer was closer to these films than any others the

Ted Pearson romances Cecilia Parker in a studio-bound beach set, with Mickey Rooney.

Lewis Stone as Judge Hardy, surrounded by Fay Holden, Cecilia Parker, Sara Haden, and Mickey Rooney

The family vacation plot now provided a convenient framework in which respectable middle-American characters could confront controversial subjects on screen, before returning to their cozy suburban refuge. The Code would allow films to allude to some bad behavior—as in the naughty Ted and Jerry characters—as long as it was ultimately rejected. Part of the charm of the series is our confidence that nothing is too dangerous for Andy. He will be safe and sound by the end of the movie, ready for the next adventure.

As for America's favorite teenager, Mickey Rooney became a household name, though he would later say there was "no connection between what you saw of Andy Hardy on the screen and what was the reality of Mickey Rooney off camera," a nod to his tumultuous personal life. He appeared in many other films at MGM, including *Babes in Arms* (1939), which paired him with his sometime Andy Hardy costar Judy Garland. The classic "let's put on a show" musical garnered him an Oscar nomination for Best Actor at the tender age of nineteen, making him still one of the youngest nominees ever in the category. He was ranked the top box-office star of 1939, 1940, and 1941 and is still well known to audiences, thanks to his long life and career. He lived until 2014, remaining a public figure well into his nineties.

studio made. He would proudly note, "You can't imagine how much good they did for America."

Film critic Kenneth Turan has approvingly called them "the squarest, corniest, most all-American gosh darn movies ever made." Their wholesome vision of adolescence is due largely to the Production Code, which began to be strictly enforced only three years earlier and, among other things, limited the scope of teenage sexuality in the movies. Thus, the rough and tumble kids in *Wild Boys of the Road* (1933) gave way to the wide-eyed and inexperienced Andy Hardy.

Summer Holiday (MGM, 1948)

With Fourth of July celebrations as the backdrop, this spirited take on young adulthood in a small town is a slice of turn-of-the-century Americana. Mickey Rooney stars as a recent high school graduate whose radical leanings clash with his family's more traditional politics. A musical remake of *Ah Wilderness!* (1935), which inspired the Hardy series, *Summer Holiday* is photographed in beautiful Technicolor and includes some innovative musical moments courtesy of seasoned director Rouben Mamoulian.

Gloria DeHaven and Mickey Rooney

MOON OVER MIAMI

Three women go gold digging in Miami Beach after losing out on an expected inheritance.

Director Walter Lang ● **Producer** Harry Joe Brown ● **Screenplay** Vincent Lawrence and Brown Holmes, adaptation by George Seaton and Lynn Starling, from the play *Three Blind Mice* by Stephen Powys

Starring **Betty Grable** Kay Latimer ● **Don Ameche** Phil McNeil
Robert Cummings Jeffrey Bolton ● **Carole Landis** Barbara Latimer
Charlotte Greenwood Aunt Susan ● **Jack Haley** Jack O'Hara

Twentieth Century-Fox, 1941 Color, 91 min.

t's always summer in Miami! Or so claimed a massive publicity campaign launched for Miami Beach in the 1920s, with huge billboards in Times Square that described the Florida town as "Where Summer Spends the Winter." The hype was enough to convince this film's three heroines that Miami was the place to see and be seen—hopefully by a wealthy man or two.

Betty Grable was certainly a woman to see, and *Moon Over Miami* marks the first time that the musical star, soon to become synonymous with her 1943 swimsuit pinup photo, had ever worn such a costume on film. Twentieth Century-Fox's vacation romance is one of the loveliest films of the era, with a Technicolor opulence that the studio perfected during the war years and a slate of exuberant new songs. The *New York Times* called *Moon Over Miami* "gaily packaged and pretty as a Fourth of July skyrocket display" when it opened in June 1941. "You can think of less pleasant ways to spend a hot Summer's eve."

The film actually begins on a warm day in Texas, where Kay Latimer (Grable) and her sister Barbara (Carole Landis) are carhops at a roadside diner that offers "service with a song." The girls work with their Aunt Susan (Charlotte Greenwood), and all three have pinned their hopes for a brighter future on a forthcoming inheritance check. But when a meager $4,000 finally

arrives, the women turn to plan B: they'll go gold digging for a wealthy husband in Miami, "where rich men are as plentiful as grapefruit and millionaires hang from every palm tree."

Soon after checking into the fashionable Flamingo Hotel and traipsing gaily through their enormous poolside bungalow, they waste no time in catching the attention of a couple of local bachelors. First is the handsome

◄◄ **Opposite page:** Don Ameche and Betty Grable, Robert Cummings and Carole Landis, Charlotte Greenwood and Jack Haley

"She was a girl next door *and* a sexpot," scholar Jeanine Basinger says of Betty Grable. "She was a girl you could take home to Mother—and hope Dad would keep his hands to himself."

Top: Betty Grable and Robert Cummings sing "You Started Something."
Bottom: Asked about Betty Grable's stardom, Debbie Reynolds remarked, "How big is big? She was the biggest."

Jeffrey Bolton (Robert Cummings), who's currently hosting a days-long party in his neighboring suite. Kay poses as a rich woman traveling with her "secretary and maid" in tow, and soon is singing and dancing with an interested Jeff and his rich friends. But he's not the only one with eyes for Kay. Phil McNeil (Don Ameche) is the heir to a steel fortune, and though he makes a bad first impression—rude, drunk, uncouth—he starts wooing Kay as well.

Jeff and Phil are opposites in more ways than one, but Kay finds herself dating them both. Part of the movie's fun is seeing the activities they enjoy together, from speedboat racing in a botanical garden to picnicking in a submarine (with scenes shot on location in Cypress Gardens and several Florida state parks).

The other highlights are the musical sequences, especially larger-scale numbers like "You Started Something," which begins with Cummings and Grable at a piano and leads to multiple rounds of song and dance, including a jaunty tap performance by the Condos Brothers. The vibrant "Kindergarten Conga" ends with an impressive turn on the dance floor by Grable and choreographer Hermes Pan.

The movie's namesake, the 1935 song "Moon Over Miami," which had been made famous by Eddy Duchin and others, appears only in instrumental form. Instead, several new songs were written by Ralph Rainger and Leo Robin, who had won an Oscar two years earlier for

Betty Grable and Don Ameche, who is credited as "Phil O'Neil" but referred to in the movie as "Phil McNeil"

"Thanks for the Memory," Bob Hope's signature tune from *The Big Broadcast of 1938*.

Grable and Ameche's previous film, *Down Argentine Way* (1940), had been such a success that Twentieth Century-Fox quickly greenlit another project for the pair. What resulted was the most lavish musical the studio had made up to that point, taking four months to film.

A previous adaptation of the same material, 1938's *Three Blind Mice*, had told of three Kansas sisters who go to California to find a rich man and starred Loretta Young, Joel McCrea, and David Niven. The decision in 1941 to switch to a South Florida setting wasn't arbitrary. A relatively modern destination, Miami wasn't even an incorporated town until a rail line was extended there in the 1890s. The first hotel in Miami Beach opened in 1915 and by the early 1920s the city was booming, thanks in part to lax enforcement of Prohibition. (For a film satirizing the land boom, see the 1929 Marx Brothers feature *The Cocoanuts*.) The bubble finally burst after a devastating hurricane in 1926—still one of the costliest in American history. Miami wouldn't fully recover until after World War II. Nevertheless, the area remained a magnet for tourists, especially northern "snowbirds" who migrated to Florida during winter months. Legendary publicist Steve Hannagan ran an effective ad campaign, telling frostbitten New Yorkers, "It's June in Miami Beach."

Primary credit for the success of *Moon Over Miami*—financial and otherwise—must go to its star. Betty Grable arrived in Hollywood in 1929 but had an unremarkable start in films as one among producer Samuel Goldwyn's chorus line of Goldwyn Girls. (One of her early movies, *The Greeks Had a Word for Them* [1932], had told a similar story to *Moon Over Miami*. Grable appears, briefly and uncredited, as a hat check girl.) Disillusioned by the late 1930s, she packed it up for Broadway. That's ironically where she was discovered by Darryl F. Zanuck, head of production at Twentieth Century-Fox, who fatefully inserted her as a last-minute replacement for Alice Faye in *Down Argentine Way*. It proved to be her breakout role, and despite a couple of serious turns in the war film *A Yank in the R.A.F.* and the film noir *I Wake Up Screaming* (both 1941), Grable soon established herself as the premier musical comedienne of the era. She was the number one box-office star of 1943 and remained in the top ten for a decade.

If any single image can account for Grable's popularity, it would undoubtedly be her famous pinup, taken by Fox studio photographer Frank Powolny during a promotional shoot for the movie *Sweet Rosie O'Grady* (1943). In it, Grable wears a white one-piece swimsuit

Vacation Inspiration

For a dose of summer any time of the year, make like Kay and head for Miami Beach. Although the original Flamingo Hotel was torn down in the 1950s, much of the island's historic Art Deco architecture—built during the recovery after the 1926 hurricane—has been preserved, and it remains Florida's most exciting coastal destination.

similar to one she has on at the end of *Moon Over Miami*. A reported two million copies were sent to GIs during the war, who decorated their barracks and bombers with her image.

One other factor elevated her to star status, reports film scholar Jeanine Basinger. "She was fabulous in color . . . Grable had real energy on the screen, and in Technicolor, the energy was electrified."

Charlotte Greenwood and Jack Haley make a perfect (and hilarious) match.

The Palm Beach Story (Paramount, 1942)

Another tale of gold digging in South Florida, this one features a determined wife (Claudette Colbert) who hopes to seduce a rich man into investing in a futuristic airport designed by her broke husband (Joel McCrea). The film is supported by Rudy Vallee and Mary Astor as a wealthy brother and sister who get financially—and romantically—involved with the main couple. The real star of the show may be the terrific screwball script by Preston Sturges, a satirical filmmaker at the peak of his career.

Joel McCrea and Claudette Colbert

STATE FAIR

An Iowa family competes for romance and blue ribbons at the annual state fair.

Director Walter Lang ● **Producer** William Perlberg ● **Screenplay** Oscar Hammerstein II, based on the novel by Philip Stong and the 1933 screenplay by Sonya Levien and Paul Green

Starring **Jeanne Crain** Margy Frake ● **Dana Andrews** Pat Gilbert
Dick Haymes Wayne Frake ● **Vivian Blaine** Emily Edwards ● **Charles Winninger** Abel Frake
Fay Bainter Melissa Frake

Twentieth Century-Fox, 1945 Color, 100 min.

A summertime tradition for many Americans is the annual fair, a mix of carnival and competition, rollicking bandstand and prizewinning livestock. The Iowa State Fair, which began in 1854, is one of the most iconic, and it serves as the setting for this homespun musical from Twentieth Century-Fox. Like *Moon Over Miami*, it was helmed by the studio's musical specialist, Walter Lang, and shot in gorgeous Technicolor, this time from noted cinematographer Leon Shamroy.

But *State Fair* is primarily understood today as part of the output of legendary songwriting team Richard Rodgers and Oscar Hammerstein II. Their recent collaboration, *Oklahoma!*, had been a major success on Broadway in 1943, and they were quickly snatched up by Fox to create their first (and only) original film score. On the surface, *State Fair* has a few obvious similarities to *Oklahoma!* Set in the nation's heartland, it celebrates the fortitude and ingenuity of country living, and it centers on a touching story of young people falling in love.

Rodgers and Hammerstein had quality material to work with, in the form of both Phil Stong's 1932 novel and Fox's 1933 film adaptation, a pre-Code drama designed as a vehicle for folksy Will Rogers and the studio's young starlet, Janet Gaynor. But the 1945 film has since become the definitive version and is arguably

◄ **Previous Page:** Dana Andrews and Jeanne Crain. *State Fair* was an adaptation of Fox's 1933 Oscar-nominated drama. In 1962, Pat Boone, Bobby Darin, and Ann-Margret would star in a Texas-set version of the musical.

Dick Haymes and Vivian Blaine confront carnival barker Harry Morgan.

the more roundly entertaining thanks to its rich musical score, beguiling cast, and striking production values.

The film opens in the small town of Brunswick, Iowa, as the Frake family prepares for a trip to the big city of Des Moines for the state fair. The parents are readying their entries for competition: Melissa (Fay Bainter) with her sour pickles and mincemeat pies, Abel (Charles Winninger) with his prized hog Blue Boy, "the finest Hampshire boar that ever breathed."

The kids, meanwhile, are both suffering. Margy (Jeanne Crain) expresses her spring fever in the Oscar-winning song "It Might as Well Be Spring." She has a perfectly suitable but unexciting fiancé, but she's nevertheless "starry eyed and vaguely discontented." We realize she's hungry for true romance, and soon she does, too. Reprising the song, she describes her ideal suitor as "a kind of handsome combination of Ronald Colman,

Jeanne Crain was a capable singer, but in *State Fair* she was dubbed by Louanne Hogan.

Charles Boyer, and Bing." Her brother Wayne (Dick Haymes) has spent the last year practicing his ring-tossing skills after having been tricked out of his money by an unscrupulous carnival barker (Harry Morgan). The film's romantic intrigue is ignited when both siblings realize they will be going to the fair without their significant others. It's a classic summer setup: away from their routine, Margy and Wayne will be challenged by new experiences and vulnerable to new love.

The casting of both young actors was a priority for the studio. Jeanne Crain was the hot newcomer, a nineteen-year-old former Miss Pan-Pacific who had earlier been spotted by Orson Welles in a studio commissary. She had unsuccessfully auditioned for *The Magnificent Ambersons* (1942), but now Darryl F. Zanuck was determined to make her a star. Haymes was already a

"It's a Grand Night for Singing," with Dana Andrews and Jeanne Crain

meets the handsome newspaper reporter Pat (Dana Andrews) on a roller coaster. By the time the orchestra starts playing "It's a Grand Night for Singing," all the characters are feeling optimistic and sing along.

It's not surprising that these rural Iowans find themselves in a different headspace, given the intoxicating atmosphere of the midway. Credit for this goes to art director Lewis Creber and supervisor Lyle Wheeler—who won five Oscars during his long career, including one for *Gone with the Wind* (1939)—along with set decorator Thomas Little.

As was customary at the time, the film's rich palette was controlled by the Technicolor Corporation, whose cofounder Natalie Kalmus was on set to supervise use of the equipment and to make sure all the colors were coordinated. The resulting look is lush, nuanced, and exceptionally warm; a soft rainbow of hues ties together the sets, costumes, and makeup. The film is awash in mid-tones—a bit of mellow orange here, a splash of rosy pink there—and has very few harsh contrasts. There is little solid white or black to be found, with even the men

recording artist with his own radio program when Fox put him under contract, taking advantage of his crooner image in musicals like *Irish Eyes Are Smiling* (1944) and *Diamond Horseshoe* (1945).

Musical performance is certainly at the heart of *State Fair*, as Wayne's new love interest turns out to be bandstand singer Emily (Vivian Blaine). Margy likewise

Vacation Inspiration

The Iowa State Fair attracts over a million visitors each August. Visit it to experience hog calling, butter sculptures, musical performances, and some of the weightiest farm animals in the country. (And every four years, lots of hopeful presidential candidates.)

dressed in gray suit jackets so as not to clash with the soothing tone of their environment. Most lovely are the film's evening scenes, when warm lighting gives everything a honeyed glow.

Film historian Richard Barrios notes that while Fox's musical output couldn't rival that of MGM, they were able to produce musical films very efficiently, resulting in some big successes. *State Fair* was the brainchild of studio chief Darryl F. Zanuck, a lover of Americana who wasn't afraid to invest in lavish detail to try to one-up his competitors. Similarities abound between *State Fair* and MGM's *Meet Me in St. Louis* (1944)—another musical about a middle-American family and an upcoming fair—which itself may have been influenced by Fox's 1933 *State Fair*.

Pedigree aside, the film remains a love letter to the integrity and resilience of everyday people, and its premiere on August 29, 1945—two weeks after the surrender of Japan, which brought World War II to a close—was perfect timing for a movie that reaffirms the American way of life.

Although the film's storyline isn't complicated, there is one early plot point that, upon its return in the final act, seems to establish the positive message of

Dana Andrews was at the peak of his career. *State Fair* was released the year in between iconic noir film *Laura* (1944) and postwar drama *The Best Years of Our Lives* (1946).

the film. Before leaving for the fair, Abel's pessimistic friend Dave (Percy Kilbride) tells him to expect disappointment in some form. "Mark my words, Abel, there's compensation in this world," he says. "For every good, there's bad." In a burst of summertime optimism, Abel wagers that not only will his hog win the top award, but his family will all have a good time at the fair and "be better for it" afterward. It's no spoiler to say that Abel wins his bet.

Carousel (Twentieth Century-Fox, 1956)

Directed by Henry King, the "King of Americana," who had helmed the 1933 version of *State Fair*, this Rodgers and Hammerstein classic is set in coastal Maine in the middle of summer—"June Is Bustin' Out All Over!" It's arguably the pair's finest musical score (which is saying something), and it features the lovely Shirley Jones as Julie Jordan and Gordon MacRae as the gruff but soulful carousel barker Billy Bigelow.

Shirley Jones and Gordon MacRae

KEY LARGO

A war veteran spends hurricane season in the Florida Keys, where he encounters a pack of gangsters.

Director John Huston ● **Producer** Jerry Wald ● **Screenplay** Richard Brooks and John Huston, based on the play by Maxwell Anderson

Starring **Humphrey Bogart** Frank McCloud ● **Edward G. Robinson** Johnny Rocco
Lauren Bacall Nora Temple ● **Lionel Barrymore** James Temple ● **Claire Trevor** Gaye Dawn

Warner Bros.,
1948
B&W, 100 min.

Nowadays, Florida is a year-round destination and summer is the high season, with many American families only available to vacation when kids are out of school. But historically, the state, and especially its southern region, was avoided during the middle of the year—it was too warm at home to worry about sweating in the tropics. But beyond the heat and humidity, the summer months come with another weather-related downside: the prevalence of hurricanes, with a five-month season of volatile storm systems that begins each year in June.

In John Huston's *Key Largo*, the oppressive summer weather works hand in hand with the drama as the hero descends, Orpheus-like, into a hellish underworld populated with unsavory figures, to save the woman he loves. This classic Warner Bros. gangster film is also a showdown between two of the studio's most iconic actors: Humphrey Bogart and Edward G. Robinson, the latter of whom gives one of his finest performances. This was the fifth and final pairing for the two Hollywood giants, and the only one for which Bogart received top billing.

At the film's opening, Bogart's character, Major Frank McCloud, arrives in Key Largo by bus. He is there to visit Nora Temple (Lauren Bacall), the young widow of a fellow soldier. She and her father-in-law, James Temple (Lionel Barrymore), run the Largo Hotel, which

◀◀ **Previous page:** Thomas Gomez aims at Humphrey Bogart. The Largo Hotel was inspired by the Caribbean Club, a fishing club—and now a bar—built in 1938 by real estate promoter Carl Fisher.

The Warner Bros. film was a box-office hit and brought notoriety to the real Key Largo.

has closed its doors for the off-season. Frank is therefore surprised to find notorious crime boss Johnny Rocco (Robinson) staying there "by special arrangement," along with a group of his henchmen and a mistress, Gaye (Claire Trevor). Having been deported to Cuba, Rocco has sneaked back into the United States and is staying at the Largo under an assumed name, with plans to sell a stash of counterfeit money.

Robinson had played the title role in *Little Caesar* (1931) seventeen years before, which launched his film career and helped popularize the gangster genre. There, his character was named Rico; here, the name Rocco isn't coincidental. The villain was devised to be an amalgam of Al Capone, who had died in Florida a few years earlier, and Charles "Lucky" Luciano, who had been deported to Cuba in 1946.

Key Largo turned out to also be the last film to costar Bogart and Bacall, whose working relationship

Lauren Bacall and Humphrey Bogart, married since 1945, made just four films together.

began with *To Have and Have Not* (1944). That Howard Hawks–directed film was similarly set at an island hotel (on Martinique) in the heat of summer, but whereas Bacall played a sly seductress in *To Have and Have Not*—made during wartime—here she plays the noble postwar role of virtuous widow and caretaker for her elderly father-in-law.

Claire Trevor had sympathy for Bacall's situation. "She was supposed to be an ordinary girl. And it's hard for Bacall to be ordinary." Meanwhile, Trevor's alcoholic gangster moll is an intriguing foil for the wholesome Nora. Her key scene is one in which Rocco forces her to perform a song before she can have a drink. When she gives a pitiful performance, Rocco refuses to pay up, propelling the compassionate Frank to pour her a shot of whiskey—his first act of defiance against the kingpin. Trevor is a knockout as Gaye, giving a convincingly world-weary performance that won her the Oscar for Best Supporting Actress.

Director John Huston had good fortune at the Academy Awards that year. In addition to Trevor's win, his earlier Warner Bros. film, *The Treasure of the Sierra Madre*, took screenplay and directing honors (both for Huston), and his father Walter won Best Supporting Actor for his portrayal of a wizened gold prospector. Warner Bros. had spent a small fortune on *Treasure*, even allowing Huston to shoot on location in Mexico, so the studio pulled in the reins on his follow-up. *Key*

Key Largo is the northernmost of the Keys and has some wonderful dive sites, including the John Pennekamp Coral Reef State Park. The island is also the current location of the thirty-five-foot steamboat used in Huston's 1951 film, *The African Queen.*

Largo was shot entirely in the soundstage, but the filmmakers did an admirable job of simulating Florida, using a large water tank for outdoor sequences.

The film was based on an antiwar stage play from 1939 by Maxwell Anderson, about a Spanish Civil War deserter. When adapting the material for a new era, Huston retained little more than the title, working with cowriter Richard Brooks to create a new storyline. On a visit to Key Largo, the pair stayed at a private fishing club that was also being operated illegally as a casino. By the time a hurricane struck, Huston and Brooks had found their story.

Very much a postwar product, *Key Largo* quotes Franklin D. Roosevelt in one scene: "We are not making all this sacrifice of human effort and human lives to return to the kind of world we had after the last World War. . . . We are fighting to cleanse the world of ancient evils, ancient ills." These words from the 1942 State of the Union Address had once motivated Frank in the war and now inspire him to fix the corruption he finds back home. Though accurately labeled a crime film, *Key Largo* was made in the heyday of both film noir and the "social problem" picture, when stories about antiheroes and society's ills were all the rage.

Given the dark subject matter, the film is appropriately shot in black and white. Cinematographer Karl Freund—an instrumental figure in the development of German Expressionism who later worked on iconic Universal horror films like *Dracula* (1931)—creates a shadowy and nightmarish atmosphere inside the hotel. The camerawork conveys the hurricane raging outside through the flickering and dimming of lights, and— along with the film's immersive sound design and practical effects like banging shutters and shattering windows—it suggests the storm raging within each of the characters.

Top: Edward G. Robinson as Johnny Rocco, the world's worst hotel guest
Bottom: Humphrey Bogart and Claire Trevor had appeared together a decade earlier in *Dead End* (1937) and *The Amazing Dr. Clitterhouse* (1938), which also starred Edward G. Robinson.

Body Heat (Warner Bros., 1981)

This neo-noir set in muggy South Florida was the first movie directed by *Raiders of the Lost Ark* (1981) screenwriter Lawrence Kasdan, and it launched the careers of its stars, William Hurt and Kathleen Turner. In an homage to noir classic *Double Indemnity* (1944), their characters begin a torrid affair and scheme to murder her husband for the insurance money. Complete with steamy love scenes that would make Bogie and Bacall blush, *Body Heat* is an engrossing mystery film that correlates the sweltering heat of a Florida summer with an eruption of passion and violence.

William Hurt and Kathleen Turner

SUMMER STOCK

A Connecticut woman opens her family farm to a group of Broadway actors for their summer production and becomes part of the show herself.

Director Charles Walters ● **Producer** Joe Pasternak ● **Screenplay** George Wells and Sy Gomberg, from a story by Sy Gomberg

Starring **Judy Garland** Jane Falbury ● **Gene Kelly** Joe Ross

Marjorie Main Esme ● **Eddie Bracken** Orville Wingait ● **Ray Collins** Jasper Wingait

Gloria DeHaven Abigail Falbury ● **Phil Silvers** Herb Blake ● **Hans Conried** Harrison Keath

MGM, 1950
Color, 109 min.

The first time we see Judy Garland, she is singing to herself in the shower: "If you feel like singing, sing!" That could be the motto for this film—the story of a young woman who comes out of her shell and becomes a star. It's a classic summer case of self-discovery.

Though live theater may customarily take a mid-year break between seasons, its performers do not. The tradition of "summer stock" theater began many decades ago as groups of actors would escape the city and head to resort towns where their regular urban audiences were vacationing. These small-town venues would give young talents a chance to hone their craft in a lower-stakes environment and let creators test new material that could someday make it to the bright lights of Broadway. Sometimes called the "straw hat circuit," summer stock had its heyday in the middle of the twentieth century. Today the romantic idea of young people putting on a show in a barn is a notion that only really exists in the movies, of which this bucolic MGM musical is the archetype.

The story opens on Falbury Farm, owned and operated by Jane Falbury (Garland). Jane is proud of her land and is especially thrilled to acquire a new red tractor from the local general store owner, Mr. Wingait (Ray Collins), whose nebbish son Orville (Eddie Bracken) has been engaged to Jane for four years. It's clear that

MGM knew the film's biggest draw was its popular leading couple.

she is in no rush to get married (she's much happier with her new tractor than with spending time with Orville), but the movie soon presents Jane with a new and more exciting love interest. Theater director Joe Ross (Gene Kelly) has unexpectedly brought his acting troupe to the farm, upon the invitation of Jane's erstwhile art-student sister Abigail (Gloria DeHaven), who has been dating

◀◀ **Previous page:** With Charles Walters standing by, Garland sits on Jane's new "Earthbuster" tractor–actually a disguised Ford 8N.

Joe in New York. They plan to set up a stage in her barn, for a summer production of Joe's musical *Fall in Love*.

In many ways the opposite of her sister, Jane is appalled by the idea of a group of artists invading her home, and she tells them to find "some other place to play." It doesn't help that they accidentally crash her new tractor. Later convinced that the troupe can be put to work on the farm, she relents and allows them to stay. Perhaps she sees some potential for herself in their show? We understand Jane as the type of girl with natural abilities—she's Judy Garland, after all—who just hasn't let her musical talents shine. "Jane's brains are in her head, not in her feet," says her no-nonsense housekeeper, Esme (Marjorie Main). But when she reluctantly dances with Joe for the first time, in the showstopping "Portland Fancy" number at the town's country dance, she proves that she is more than capable of joining their ranks. It's obvious that she and Joe have romantic potential, too.

Though summer stock theater is about big city performers bringing their skills to small-town audiences, here it is presented as the film's central conflict. On one side is Jane, the noble farmer who tills the earth and puts her own food on her table. On the other side are the big city folk who, she assumes, have never done a

Top: Broadway actors overrun the Falbury family farm.
Middle: Phil Silvers and Gene Kelly tell the troupe to "Dig Dig Dig Dig for Your Dinner."
Bottom: Kelly supported Garland both on screen and off. Charles Walters recalled, "He'd placate Judy and hold her hand, asking, 'Anything I can do today?'"

Eddie Bracken and Judy Garland talk love and farm equipment.

hard day's work. "This is a farm, this isn't Broadway," she tells Abigail. "These people just don't belong here." But they win her over by showing their willingness to work hard; she wins them over by singing and dancing with the best of them. Representing two cultures coming together, *Summer Stock* is a mixture of the folk musical, which genre scholar Rick Altman describes as "everyday Americans going about their business" ("Howdy Neighbor, Happy Harvest!"), and the backstage musical, which is typically set behind the scenes of the theatrical world.

By 1950, MGM was feeling the pinch from television. With weekly movie attendance down 25 percent in the previous five years, Louis B. Mayer's old-fashioned studio was canceling a lot of its "B" film franchises, including the once-popular Andy Hardy and Thin Man series, and trying to adapt to changing audience tastes. Some notable exceptions to MGM's industrial challenges were the musicals coming out of the Arthur Freed and Joe Pasternak production units.

A producer of hit Deanna Durbin films at Universal in the 1930s, Pasternak came to MGM in 1941 to work on musical pictures with stars like Kathryn Grayson, Esther Williams, and Gene Kelly. Pasternak assigned studio choreographer and Garland's former on-screen dance partner, Charles Walters, to direct *Summer Stock*. Walters had provided dance direction for the 1943 musical *Girl Crazy*, the last film in which Garland and Mickey Rooney performed on screen together, and *Summer Stock* was intended as a vehicle to reunite the popular duo—until Rooney was abruptly released from his contract and replaced by Kelly.

Walters would later claim that making the film was "absolute torture." This was the era of Judy Garland's most erratic behavior behind the scenes, a result of her dependence on prescription medications and chronic insecurities about her appearance, after more than a decade of being overworked and treated recklessly by the studio. Now at only age twenty-seven, she was frequently absent from set and difficult to work with. Though *Summer Stock* would be her last film at MGM, and one of the final starring musical roles

Many well-established summer playhouses are still in operation, especially in New England, where *Summer Stock* is set. If there's not a summer stock theater near you, try supporting your local community theater. You may just discover Broadway's next star.

Top: Gloria DeHaven and Gene Kelly take a break from farm work, to the dismay of Marjorie Main and Judy Garland.
Bottom: The famous "Get Happy" sequence was shot two months after production wrapped. Garland told director Charles Walters, "I want to wear the costume from the 'Mr. Monotony' number cut from *Easter Parade* (1948). And I want you to do it."

of her career, none of her troubles are apparent on screen. She remains, characteristically, a remarkable and captivating performer.

How fitting, then, that the film's most famous number, Garland's iconic performance of "Get Happy," asks the audience to "Forget your troubles, come on, get happy! / You better chase all your cares away!" This dynamic sequence was included as a final payoff scene for Jane, the young farmer who became a musical star over the course of the summer, with a song written years earlier by Harold Arlen, the composer of Garland's signature tune, "Over the Rainbow."

Of course, the film wouldn't be what it is without its terrific supporting cast. Of note is comedian Phil Silvers as the gregarious actor and stagehand Herb, whom Walters intentionally emphasized for comic relief. Gene Kelly, ever the consummate performer, plays a somewhat rougher version of his typically suave persona. Yet he does some of his best dancing here, including a solo in which he interacts with the empty barn stage, prancing on a squeaky floorboard and a stray sheet of newspaper. Kelly has a masculine, athletic presence, and despite the effortless grace with which he dances, it's no stretch to think of him hoisting lumber and hammering nails inside a barn on a hot summer's day.

Make It a Double Feature

Floating Weeds (Daiei Film, 1959)

Set a world away, Japanese director Yasujiro Ozu's tale of a traveling theater troupe presents a similar conflict between a group of out-of-town actors and the villagers who host them. The central character is an elderly Kabuki actor who visits a former mistress, with whom he secretly has a young son. This beautifully crafted and contemplative film is thoroughly accessible, even for those weaned on MGM musicals. Film critic Roger Ebert was a particular fan, praising the atmosphere of a small-town summer "where the heat and the quiet have created a kind of dreamy suspension of the rules."

Hiroshi Kawaguchi and Ganjiro Nakamura

MONSIEUR HULOT'S HOLIDAY

The charmingly clumsy Mr. Hulot spends a week at a seaside hotel and causes a series of humorous mishaps.

Director Jacques Tati ● **Producer** Fred Orain ● **Screenplay** Jacques Tati and Henri Marquet, with the collaboration of Pierre Aubert and Jacques Lagrange

Starring **Jacques Tati** Monsieur Hulot ● **Nathalie Pascaud** Martine ● **Micheline Rolla** The Aunt ● **Raymond Carl** Waiter ● **Lucien Frégis** Hotel Proprietor ● **André Dubois** Commandant

Discifilm (France), 1953 B&W, 87 min.

At its most basic level, *Monsieur Hulot's Holiday* is about a leisurely week at the beach. Bursting from the mind of French director and star Jacques Tati, one of the cinema's great physical comedians, it becomes an amusing series of slapstick, sight gags, and humorous escapades. Whereas a typical film will contain an overarching story, characters with motivations, and a set of dramatic conflicts that are resolved by the end, Tati throws out the standard cause-and-effect structure and replaces it with comedic vignettes that make up not so much a story but a low-key vaudeville show. Who Hulot is and why he is at this beach are never revealed, nor do we know where he lives or works. There is no love interest. When the film opened in the United States in 1954, a *New York Times* film critic described him simply as an "amiable butterfingered nitwit bouncing around a summer hotel."

Tati's character is a sweet-natured outsider, eternally curious but not full of comprehension. He stands apart from other comedic icons like Chaplin's mischievous Tramp and Harold Lloyd's bespectacled go-getter. Hulot has no intention of causing havoc (though his nosiness often gets the best of him), nor does he tug at heartstrings. Tati describes Hulot as "human, simple, shy. Someone you might meet walking down the street and not think he's a comic character from a movie."

◀◀ **Previous page:** Jacques Tati and Nathalie Pascaud dance at the hotel's masquerade party.

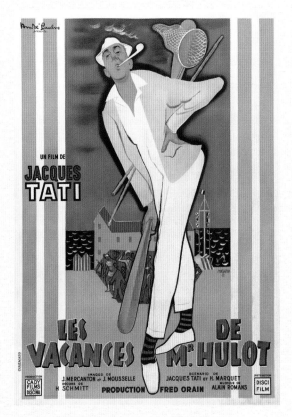

The original French poster for *Les Vacances de Monsieur Hulot*

Despite its charms, *Monsieur Hulot's Holiday* is a relatively unemotional film precisely because the main character remains at a distance. We might feel sorry for his blunders, but we don't worry about him. Much of the reason for this is the objective attitude that the film takes. The camera never gets too close—in case Hulot may knock it over?—which also serves to give the humor a dry quality. If it weren't full of silliness, you might assume *Monsieur Hulot's Holiday* was a vérité documentary, because the camera simply observes the behavior of the beachgoers.

A great example of this style is in the opening scene, set at a train station where people are heading out of town on holiday. Confused about which platform to occupy, a frenzied crowd rushes from one track to another, en masse. Instead of following them through the tunnels, the camera simply sits still, taking in the movements of the crowd from a distance. The camera's role is observer, not participant; if the characters look ridiculous, it's on them.

Jacques Tati starred as Hulot in four films. The character also made a cameo appearance in François Truffaut's *Bed and Board* (1970).

This sets the mood for the bumbling Hulot, who, instead of reaching the seashore via train, sputters along in an old, tiny car. The lobby of his hotel is full of guests, and when he opens the door it lets in a strong breeze, blowing a man's long mustache across his face and causing tea to pour at odd angles from its pot. People cling to their hats, newspapers go fluttering. Hulot enters, pipe in mouth, blissfully unaware of the disturbance he's caused.

An early beach gag involves a man painting a name onto his sailboat. The chain holding the boat in place is suddenly knocked loose and it slides down into the water while the man is mid-stroke, smearing black paint along the hull. Hulot stands nearby, innocently toweling off as the boat's owner eyes him suspiciously. Guilty or not (it's left unclear), there are never any serious ramifications for Hulot's blunders. He just goes amiably on to the next situation. Soon he's aggravating folks on the tennis court with his unorthodox serve and, later, accidentally detonates a shed full of fireworks.

Of course, unfortunate things do happen to Hulot from time to time. When he goes out for a ride in a kayak, the shoddy vessel splits in half, folding up over itself and trapping him inside. As he struggles to escape, onlookers gawk from the beach.

Rather than feeling slight, the movie's simplicity is aligned with its theme of disconnecting from one's everyday routine—or the inability to do so. "A man goes

Top: Hulot's unfortunate kayak outing
Middle: Jacques Tati, Micheline Rolla, and Nathalie Pascaud spend their day on the beach.
Bottom: Lucien Frégis as the frustrated hotel proprietor, with Jacques Tati

on vacation and thinks everyone around him wants to enjoy their vacation too," Tati explained. "But we soon see . . . none of these people are really on vacation." A businessman checks his stock portfolio, a retired military commander recounts his war experiences, a young intellectual bemoans the bourgeoisie, the radio broadcast in the hotel lobby reminds listeners of the ongoing conflict in Southeast Asia. It becomes clear that many people are incapable of enjoying a vacation because of the preoccupations of modern life. The fact that we know little about Hulot's personal or professional life seems to be the point. *Monsieur Hulot's Holiday* is about what summer vacation should be: a true escape, one in which the problems of the real world do not enter. It's also a reminder to his fellow citizens of the social benefits introduced by the Popular Front government of the 1930s, which mandated paid holidays for French workers and resulted in a flood of tourism. The film presents leisure time, almost twenty years later, as a French right.

Jacques Tati, born with the Russian surname Tatischeff, started out as a music hall performer, doing pantomime and satirical imitations. He moved to film because of the greater resources and possibilities of the medium. "You can do things in films that are impossible on a stage," he recounted. *Monsieur Hulot's Holiday* (originally released in the United States as *Mr. Hulot's Holiday*) was his second film, after *Jour de Fête* (1949), in which he played a small-town postman. But it was the first appearance of the beloved Hulot, who would appear in three more features: *Mon Oncle* (1958), about the modern home, winner of the Oscar for Best Foreign Language Film; *Playtime* (1967), about the modern city; and *Trafic* (1971), about modern car culture. Each of these depicts Hulot as a fish out of water, an old school Frenchman who struggles to make sense of a mechanized and less humane world. He is continually bemused by the changes happening around him, and the films suggest that modern living isn't all it's cracked up to be.

Vacation Inspiration

Monsieur Hulot's Holiday was shot at a real hotel located in the town of Saint-Marc-sur-Mer, on France's Atlantic coast. It's now the Best Western Hotel de la Plage, and it—along with the neighboring beach—plays up its connection to the famous film. There's even a statue of Hulot, which gazes across the beach toward the sea.

A Day in the Country (Panthéon, 1936)

Jean Renoir, another iconic French filmmaker and son of Impressionist painter Pierre-Auguste Renoir, follows a family into the countryside for a leisurely afternoon picnic. Their day trip gets interrupted by a couple of amorous young men who have eyes for the women of the party. Made in 1936, just as mandatory paid holidays were being introduced in France, it revels in the beauty of nature and the pleasure of escape. Renoir, a master of humanism, studies how people's behavior and inclinations can change when away from their everyday routine.

Sylvia Bataille

REAR WINDOW

A man spies on his neighbors during a hot New York summer, suspecting one of murder.

Director Alfred Hitchcock ● **Producer** Alfred Hitchcock ● **Screenplay** John Michael Hayes, based on the short story "It Had to Be Murder" by Cornell Woolrich

**Paramount, 1954
Color, 112 min.**

Starring **James Stewart** L. B. "Jeff" Jefferies ● **Grace Kelly** Lisa Fremont ● **Thelma Ritter** Stella ● **Raymond Burr** Lars Thorwald ● **Wendell Corey** Tom Doyle ● **Judith Evelyn** Miss Lonelyhearts ● **Ross Bagdasarian** The Songwriter ● **Georgine Darcy** Miss Torso

Some films simply couldn't take place at another time of year. If not for the summer swelter—made obvious by occasional cutaways to a wall thermometer—L. B. Jefferies (James Stewart) wouldn't have had his windows open, inviting him to gaze out at his neighbors and speculate on their lives. He wouldn't have been able to hear the piano music coming from a songwriter's apartment, and he certainly wouldn't have been eyeing up a scantily clad young woman across the courtyard. And is it just the heat playing tricks on his mind, or has Lars Thorwald been acting suspiciously lately?

This summertime mystery originated in the 1942 short story "It Had to Be Murder" by Cornell Woolrich. When the bare-bones story was adapted into a screenplay, a romantic subplot was added, as were several minor characters, like "Miss Torso" (Georgine Darcy) and chatty therapist Stella (Thelma Ritter).

Before beginning work on the script, writer John Michael Hayes knew that the film would star Stewart and Grace Kelly, and the parts were scripted with those actors in mind. The reason for casting Stewart was simple: "Jimmy represented to the audience the ordinary man," explains Patricia Hitchcock, the director's daughter. Hayes wrote the everyman character as a photojournalist, someone who typically remains behind the scenes, a recorder of visual information. Grace Kelly's

Lisa, an actress in a previous version of the screenplay, was transformed into a fashion model, which suggests how she would have met Jeff. Alfred Hitchcock described her as "a typical active New York woman," and he considered the elegant, blonde Grace Kelly an ideal heroine for his films.

Stella was written to provide a "broad, coarse vaudeville kind of humor," according to Hayes, who wanted to bring the audience together in laughter before suspense

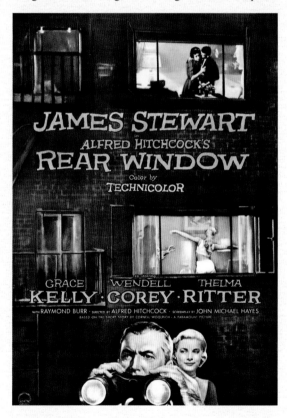

Rear Window was a box-office hit in 1954 and remains one of Hitchcock's most beloved films.

◄ **Previous page:** Jeff (Jimmy Stewart) feels more comfortable behind the camera.

and shock. A typical moment occurs when she wonders aloud how Thorwald (Raymond Burr) could have "cut up" his wife—all the while leaning over Jeff, who's trying to eat his breakfast with a knife and fork.

Although it's a believable New York, the outdoor set was actually built entirely indoors, on Stage 18 of the Paramount lot in Hollywood. Art director Joseph MacMillan Johnson designed and built the courtyard, digging out the soundstage's basement level at production designer Henry Bumstead's suggestion. This allowed the set to be built to scale, including a total of thirty-one apartments, twelve of which had furnishings and workable plumbing.

The environment therefore feels—and indeed, is—lived-in by Jeff's neighbors, and because of the balmy summer weather, people are out and about, interacting with each other to an unusual degree. The distance between actors meant that Hitchcock would give each one direction with the use of an earpiece. But he was also able to record the sounds of their apartments from Jeff's perspective, which lends the film an added sense of spatial realism. We see them, hear them, and come to know them just as Jeff would.

There's the songwriter (Ross Bagdasarian) who struggles with a new tune throughout the film, and the woman Jeff nicknames "Miss Lonelyhearts" (Judith Evelyn), who hears his music when she most needs it. A pair of newlyweds spend most of the time with their

Top: Jimmy Stewart and his neighbors keep their windows open during a balmy New York summer.
Bottom: Raymond Burr, likely thinking, "This weather is murder."

shades modestly drawn, while Miss Torso bounces freely around her open apartment. A couple sleep on their fire escape to stay cool, occasionally lowering their small dog to the courtyard in a basket.

Rear Window is set in Greenwich Village, but it was shot entirely on a Hollywood set. Today you can visit the Paramount lot along with many other studios in the Los Angeles area. You'll see where all the magic is made, from the soundstages holding entire courtyards to the streets of New York made of simple facades.

In his review of *Rear Window*, François Truffaut described Hitchcock as the kind of director who makes his movies with "the public in mind," meaning their success or failure depends on the audience's reaction. To this end, Hitchcock's movies are both highly engaging and full of manipulation; we are meant to experience things just as the director wants us to, and to feel just as he wants us to feel. Hitchcock famously made extensive use of storyboards, planning each moment for a specific effect; he later called the time on set "boring," because he had already completed the film in his head by the time the cameras started to roll.

Critics have suggested that Jeff is "a Hitchcock surrogate" who sits in his chair with a camera, looking at strangers and inventing stories about them. Like turning a television dial, he flips between channels as he moves his lens from apartment to apartment. The exercise turns dangerous when he becomes wrapped up in his creation. The moment when Thorwald looks back at Jeff is blood-chilling because it crosses a terrifying line, where Jeff's voyeurism suddenly has real-world consequences.

Alternatively, *Rear Window* can be understood as a romance undergoing a stress test. Jeff and Lisa begin the film at an impasse: because of her urban sophistication and haute couture, Jeff stubbornly thinks she's not cut out for the rugged life he leads. Before there's any hint of a murder plot, the film becomes preoccupied with Jeff's love life. He tells his boss that getting married would be a "drastic" move; Stella gives him a lecture on how "maladjusted misfits" can create a wonderful life together. The romantic intrigue is so overt as to suggest that the murder plotline is really at the service of the film's biggest mystery: will Jeff and Lisa get married?

Though it's a bit condescending—the woman ultimately must prove to the man that she's more than just a pretty face—the love story gives color to the rest of the film. Consider that Thorwald's marriage is a cautionary tale for the unmarried Jeff, who worries about what it would mean to have a "nagging" wife. Having made a career out of keeping himself at a distance and observing, camera in hand, Jeff would prefer to stay out of emotional commitments; he rebuffs the advances of

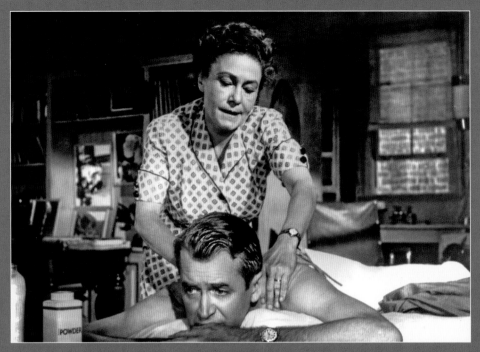

Top: Thelma Ritter gives Jimmy Stewart a massage and a dose of common sense.
Bottom: "Is this the Lisa Fremont who never wears the same dress twice?" asks Jeff. "Only because it's expected of her," she replies.

the one person in his life who wants to look back at him. The last time he got too close to his subject, it left him with a broken leg.

But we know Jeff is hooked when Lisa returns from Thorwald's apartment, high on adrenaline after delivering a threatening note. Suddenly she's speaking Jeff's language, and he sees her as a woman he might not have to just "settle down" with, because she'd be up for an adventure, too. He gives a wondrous smile. By crossing the courtyard, Lisa has become one of the characters in his murder mystery diorama. It gives a whole new meaning to the song "To See You Is to Love You."

Make It a Double Feature

To Catch a Thief (Paramount, 1955)

The year after *Rear Window*, Hitchcock made this stylish thriller about a jewel thief, set in the romantic French Riviera with Grace Kelly and the ever-appealing Cary Grant. The two leads share a wonderful chemistry, and they're supported by a screenplay full of tantalizing innuendo. Shot on location in Cannes, the film defines picturesque and took home an Oscar for its cinematography.

Grace Kelly and Cary Grant

SUMMERTIME

An Ohio school secretary arrives in Venice, where she falls for a handsome antiques salesman (and into a canal).

Director David Lean ● **Producer** Ilya Lopert ● **Screenplay** H. E. Bates and David Lean, based on the play *The Time of the Cuckoo* by Arthur Laurents

Starring **Katharine Hepburn** Jane Hudson ● **Rossano Brazzi** Renato de Rossi
Gaetano Autiero Mauro ● **Isa Miranda** Signora Fiorini ● **Jane Rose** Edith McIlhenny
MacDonald Parke Lloyd McIlhenny ● **Darren McGavin** Eddie Yaeger ● **Mari Aldon** Phyl Yaeger

United Artists,
1955
Color, 100 min.

n the opening scene of *Summertime*, Jane Hudson (Katharine Hepburn) crosses the lagoon into the storybook city of Venice, Italy, on the last leg on her solo European vacation. With guidebook and 8mm movie camera in hand, she negotiates her way onto a vaporetto where she meets the McIlhennys (MacDonald Parke and Jane Rose), a retired American couple who are also enjoying their first trip abroad. At her hotel, a small pensione run by a war widow (Isa Miranda), she encounters a young painter and his wife (Darren McGavin and Mari Aldon). These characters represent an assortment of relationships: two single women—one by choice—and two childless couples, one in its early stages and another at the end of a long marriage. Since Jane is alone, it feels inevitable that she will have her own summer affair in this most romantic of destinations. After all, she's come to Venice "to find what she'd been missing all her life."

In the years after the war, Hollywood was making more and more "runaway productions"—films shot on location outside the United States. It became commonplace in the 1950s to see stories of Americans in Europe—particularly young, often naive, women who visit for the summer, take in the culture, and find themselves involved with amorous European men who have a less repressed attitude about love. Twentieth Century-Fox's popular *Three Coins in the Fountain* (1954) was

◀◀ **Previous page:** Katharine Hepburn waits for love, with her Italian phrasebook.

Hepburn and Venice were the film's twin attractions. *Summertime* was later released as *Summer Madness* in the UK.

one such movie, a story of three single women shot on the streets of Rome. Film scholar Robert Shandley writes that these "European travelogue romances . . . provide an insight into America's evolving sense of its place in the wider world of the postwar era."

Director David Lean was therefore accommodated when he asked to shoot *Summertime* on location. Lean's introduction to Venice had been as the editor of the film *Escape Me Never* (1935), for which exteriors had been shot in the city; he paid his first visit there after the film was completed. Historian Kevin Brownlow notes that *Summertime* was "David's favorite film, starring his favorite actress," set in "one of his favorite places in the world." Venice certainly does a number on cynical Lloyd McIlhenny, who upon his arrival dismisses it as "Luna Park on water" and gripes to his wife, "If I have to look at one more painting, I'll yip." Days later he enthusiastically tells Jane that she must visit the Academy of Fine Arts: "Rooms full of pictures!" he raves.

Though she's traveling alone, Jane puts up a brave face. "I'm the independent type," she says. "Always have

Katharine Hepburn and Rossano Brazzi share a romantic evening.

been." As she wanders around Venice taking photos, her only companion a nosey street urchin named Mauro (Gaetano Autiero), she seems to be getting lonelier and more self-conscious. One day she visits an antique shop where a beautiful red goblet catches her eye—as does the handsome shop owner. He is the suave Renato de Rossi (Rossano Brazzi), with whom she soon embarks on a romance. There's a lot she doesn't know about him (and vice versa) and part of the film's drama lies in how they come to terms with each other, the American school secretary and the dashing Italian playboy.

In a sense, her romantic fling with the young Venetian is another part of Jane's cultural immersion—a special perk her travel agent may have promised about Europe, along with hearing the chimes of Big Ben and watching the sunset from the Eiffel Tower. Renato could wind up being just another story she'll share with friends

Katharine Hepburn on location with David Lean, who remarked of *Summertime*, "I've put more of myself in that film than in any other I've ever made."

Top: Jane (Katharine Hepburn) and her local tour guide, Mauro (Gaetano Autiero)
Bottom: Rossano Brazzi as Renato

back in Ohio. But her transition from lone explorer to enraptured lover—captured in a sequence in which she gets a makeover and buys a new outfit for their date—stands in opposition to the impersonal, packaged itinerary of the McIlhennys, whose agenda allows them the occasional two-hour window for "independent activity." Which travel style will reap the most cultural rewards? Jane's approach is riskier, but it results in moments of exhilaration, and even fireworks.

Romance aside, the film has other memorable and humorous moments, including a famous scene in which Jane accidentally falls into a canal while filming with her 8mm camera. When the locals help pull her out, she quips, "You should have seen me in the Olympics!"

In fact, Katharine Hepburn reportedly would swim in the canals during the shoot in Venice. She had been a natural choice to play Jane and was hired even before the screenplay was written. Rossano Brazzi, who was about to become famous as an Italian charmer in both *Three Coins in the Fountain* and *The Barefoot Contessa* (1954), met Lean during a casting search in Italy. In

Vacation Inspiration

There's no place in the world like Venice. Find a classic pensione near San Marco and experience the city that seems to exist out of time. Though it's a maze of narrow alleys and waterways, Venice is compact and perfect for wandering, just as Jane does. Just try not to fall into a canal.

addition to the authentic location shoot, most of the crew were Italian, as were the cameras: they had been rented from Rome's Cinecittà Studios.

British producer Alexander Korda implored Lean to not be like one of those "artsy" directors who avoided clichéd images of Venice. "They're not cliché for nothing," Korda told him, and encouraged him to include shots of the Grand Canal and the Piazza San Marco. Lean would call these "eyefuls" and challenged himself to photograph them in new and interesting ways. He was also a perfectionist, and his methodical process—along with the challenges of moving equipment around on barges and packs of tourists trying to get a glimpse of Hepburn—led to a lengthy shoot.

The film had been based on the 1952 play *The Time of the Cuckoo* by Arthur Laurents, who would later adapt it into the 1965 musical *Do I Hear a Waltz?* with music by Richard Rodgers and lyrics by Stephen Sondheim. Certain story elements had been altered for Lean's film, including Brazzi's character, who had been much coarser and unrefined in the original material. Hepburn reportedly told Laurents after the film was completed, "You won't like it. But I'm brilliant." He didn't. She was.

Make It a Double Feature

Shirley Valentine (Paramount, 1989)

"This year Greece. Next year the world." So says Shirley, a bored English housewife who fantasizes about escaping her daily drudgery. She eventually does just that, flying to Greece and transforming her "unused life" into one she's only dreamed of, including a fling with a local tavern owner. Having starred in the original play, Tony winner and Oscar nominee Pauline Collins gives a vulnerable and warmhearted performance as a woman remaking her life in one of the world's most beautiful settings.

Pauline Collins

THE SEVEN YEAR ITCH

When his family leaves him alone for the summer, a New York man becomes obsessed with the beautiful woman upstairs.

Director Billy Wilder ● **Producers** Charles K. Feldman and Billy Wilder
Screenplay George Axelrod and Billy Wilder, based on the play by Axelrod

Starring **Tom Ewell** Richard Sherman ● **Marilyn Monroe** The Girl
Evelyn Keyes Helen Sherman ● **Sonny Tufts** Tom MacKenzie ● **Robert Strauss** Mr. Kruhulik
Oskar Homolka Dr. Brubaker ● **Marguerite Chapman** Miss Morris

Twentieth Century-Fox, 1955 Color, 105 min.

The disappointing truth about summer is that some people must continue to work while others take off on relaxing vacations. Here's a film about how to make the most of your time in the city when, say, your family is out of town and the apartment upstairs is being sublet by a blonde bombshell. Best known for a publicity stunt—Marilyn Monroe's white skirt blowing up over a subway grate, an image that once graced Times Square in a fifty-two-foot advertisement for the film—it's fair to say that *The Seven Year Itch* is all about its leading actress. The first time she appears on screen, the movie comes alive, and while it may not be considered one of Billy Wilder's best films (an incredibly high bar), it is nevertheless a must-see for its iconic depiction of a Hollywood legend. It's also just plain summer fun.

As the movie tells it, the seven-year itch is a romantic discontentment that strikes in the seventh year of marriage. The one itching in this case is publishing executive Richard Sherman (Tom Ewell), who in the opening sequence sends his wife (Evelyn Keyes) and young son (Tom Nolan) off to Maine for the summer while he stays in the city to work. He promises to behave himself, and that first night eats at a health food restaurant, locks away his cigarettes, and substitutes soda pop for his usual cocktail.

◄◄ **Opposite page:** Marilyn Monroe as the Girl, a role originated on stage by Vanessa Brown

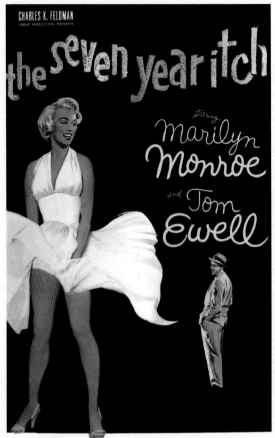

The Seven Year Itch was adapted from the hit play that ran an impressive 1,141 performances on Broadway.

But then he meets his upstairs neighbor. Monroe's character here is twenty-two and not very sophisticated;

The iconic image of Marilyn Monroe, this moment was captured both on Lexington Ave. in Manhattan (left) as a publicity stunt and later in the studio (above) for the final film.

she's the kind of girl who dips potato chips in champagne. Because he's awestruck by her beauty—or rather, overcome with lust—it never occurs to Richard to ask her name. In fact, she's simply credited as "the Girl." The pair begin to spend lots of time together, both aware that their relationship could be easily misconstrued. The other men of the film seem to take adultery as a given. Even the building's janitor, Mr. Kruhulik (Robert Strauss), goads Richard on: "Come now, Mr. Sherman. We're both summer bachelors. Don't let's be naive."

What had been an outright sexual affair in the original stage production of *The Seven Year Itch* was—due to Production Code restrictions—reduced to a chaste friendship on screen, with salacious aspects present

only in Richard's vivid imagination. We see his inner thoughts so often that in certain scenes—when Richard's jealous wife comes back wielding a gun, or when the Girl appears through a trap door in the ceiling—it's not immediately clear what is real and what is imagined. Blame it on the summer heat.

Indeed, the movie makes frequent reference to the seasonal weather, starting with his wife's explanation to their son that "poor Daddy has to stay in the hot city and make money." Richard proudly tells the Girl that he has air-conditioning in every room, and she reveals that, when it's really warm out, she keeps her "undies in the icebox." After Mr. Kruhulik mentions having a bit of summertime infidelity, Richard exclaims, "Some-

The lesson of the film may be to spend the summer outside of the city, but even during the hottest months New York has much to offer, including some of the greatest museums in the world (with air-conditioning!) and the well-shaded Central Park. If you still can't stay cool, visit the subway grate at Lexington and 52nd Street—it worked for Marilyn!

thing happens to people in this town in the summer—it's disgraceful!"

Despite being one of cinema's most captivating stars, Monroe rarely gets the credit she deserves as an actress and is often dismissed as simply a "dumb blonde" type. (The *New York Times* reviewer said "she doesn't have to act in a picture, she just has to wiggle.") But she gives one of her most charming and sensitive performances here as the Girl, who is revealed in a late monologue to be particularly astute about men. Billy Wilder deserves credit for his deft direction of Monroe, and he would later be responsible for perhaps her finest role, that of Sugar Kane Kowalczyk in *Some Like It Hot* (1959).

Wilder wrote, produced, and directed *The Seven Year Itch* but had up to this point primarily made more dramatic films. By 1955, he was most known for the noir *Double Indemnity* (1944); his Oscar-winning depiction of alcoholism, *The Lost Weekend* (1945); and his scathing Hollywood critique, *Sunset Boulevard* (1950). His previous film was *Sabrina* (1954), starring Audrey

Hepburn as the object of multiple men's affections. Though *The Seven Year Itch* is highly watchable and endlessly charming, one Wilder biographer describes it as "popular, funny, and very thin . . . one of Wilder's weakest films." Whether or not that's a fair assessment, it should be noted that weak Wilder is better than many filmmakers' good work.

One problem is that the movie's script, based on the play by co-screenwriter George Axelrod, feels inevitably stage bound. In a conceit that certainly worked better in a live theater, Richard speaks aloud much of his inner monologue; this helps move the story along in the film but simultaneously feels forced and unnatural. Axelrod suggests, "The claustrophobic element of the play is what makes it work [on stage]. The guy trapped in the little apartment, his imagination soaring out. When you open up the play, it loses its tension."

Wilder reportedly wasn't a fan of Axelrod's play to begin with. The playwright had idolized the filmmaker, but legend has it that when Axelrod brought a copy of

Top: "I figured it just isn't right to drink champagne in matador pants," says the Girl. "Would you mind fastening my straps in the back?"
Bottom: Tom Ewell falls for (and with) Marilyn Monroe.

his play to their first meeting, Wilder dropped it to the floor and said, "We'll use it as a doorstop."

Nevertheless, when the play had opened on Broadway in 1952, it became extremely successful, running for more than a thousand performances. When it started drawing the attention of film studios, the *Hollywood Reporter* dubbed it "lust weekend," a reference to Wilder's earlier film. There's even a mention of the play in *Sabrina*, when Humphrey Bogart's character asks his secretary to secure him tickets to the show. Tom Ewell played the original role on Broadway and won a Tony Award for it. Much like Monroe's "dumb blonde" persona, Ewell would forever be identified as his character here, the bumbling summer bachelor.

Out of the Blue (Eagle-Lion, 1947)

A husband (George Brent) winds up alone in the city after his wife of seven years (Carole Landis) takes a train out of town to visit her sister. He soon runs into a single and slightly nutty woman (Ann Dvorak) who takes an obsessive liking to him. Essentially a screwball combination of *The Seven Year Itch* and *Rear Window*, the story is complete with a neighboring artist-playboy and a serial killer on the loose in Greenwich Village.

Turhan Bey and Virginia Mayo

PICNIC

A drifter seduces a local girl during a Kansas town's Labor Day celebration.

Director Joshua Logan ● **Producer** Fred Kohlmar ● **Screenplay** Daniel Taradash,
based on the play by William Inge

Starring **William Holden** Hal Carter ● **Kim Novak** Madge Owens
Rosalind Russell Rosemary Sydney ● **Susan Strasberg** Millie Owens
Cliff Robertson Alan Benson ● **Arthur O'Connell** Howard Bevans
Betty Field Flo Owens ● **Verna Felton** Helen Potts ● **Nick Adams** Bomber

Columbia, 1955
Color, 115 min.

"Nobody works today! It's Labor Day!" says Mrs. Potts (Verna Felton) when drifter Hal Carter (William Holden) arrives at her doorstep seeking employment. Hal is in Kansas to see an old college friend, Alan Benson (Cliff Robertson), who lives in the fashionable end of town with his father (Raymond Bailey), owner of the local grain elevators that seem to loom in the film's background. Hal meets the Owens family: single mother Flo (Betty Field) and her two daughters. Millie (Susan Strasberg) is the young tomboy, more interested in books than boys; Madge (Kim Novak) is the beautiful elder, who has been dating Alan for the summer. The two girls are often at odds—or more precisely, jealous of each other. "What good is it just to be pretty?" Madge asks. "Maybe I get tired of only being looked at."

Rooming at the Owens's home is Rosemary (Rosalind Russell), an unmarried schoolteacher. She's the first to notice the virile Hal, who strips off his shirt while doing chores in Mrs. Potts's yard. She complains aloud, but clearly enjoys the show.

Labor Day, the traditional endpoint of summer and beginning of the new school year, became a federal holiday in 1894, the heyday of the early labor movement. Here it represents not just a day on the calendar, but an awakening for the love-starved women of the

◄◄ **Opposite page:** The entire cast unites for the Labor Day picnic, a sequence the *New York Times* called "inventive, eye-catching, and eye-filling."

Picnic had earned the 1953 Pulitzer Prize for Drama for playwright William Inge.

town and a moment of crisis for Madge and her family. The film's centerpiece is the annual picnic, which starts in the afternoon and is full of traditional outdoor events: a three-legged race, a pie-eating contest, a talent show at the bandstand. Rendered spiritedly by director Joshua Logan, the picnic sequence was described by *Time* magazine as "a wonderfully splashy mess of cinematic mulligatawny."

William Holden and Kim Novak slow dance to "Moonglow."

The key scene, and the one that made the film so immediately famous, is the lantern-lit, riverside dance between Madge and Hal, where the two share an entrancingly intimate moment before Hal's shirt gets accidentally ripped apart—a symbol of the primal instincts he represents. Madge is deeply affected by their slow dance in the warm summer air; the scene is the closest a film could come to carnal knowledge in 1955.

The stage production of *Picnic*, written by Kansas native William Inge, had opened in February 1953 on Broadway and won the Pulitzer Prize for Drama. Inge, who has been dubbed the "Playwright of the Midwest," said he wanted to write a play that took place "in the sunshine" and had considered giving it an alternate title—*Women in Summer*—because "it recalled something to me: a memory of women, all sorts of women—beautiful, bitter, harsh, loving, young, old, frustrated, happy—sitting on a front porch on a summer evening." *Picnic*'s

success on stage was perfect timing for Columbia Pictures. In the late 1940s, studio head Harry Cohn had begun to scoop up more and more properties from Broadway, starting with an adaptation of *Born Yesterday* (1950). The studio went on to produce film versions of *Death of a Salesman* (1951), *Pal Joey* (1957), and *Bell, Book and Candle* (1958), among others.

Kim Novak, the star of several of these films, had been plucked from obscurity and signed to Columbia in the early 1950s. Her first major role was what ads called the "hot-blooded blonde" opposite Fred MacMurray in the noir film *Pushover* (1954). Cohn took a special interest in Novak, recognizing in her the perfect mix of glamour and vulnerability. Meanwhile, William Holden was at the peak of his popularity. Billy Wilder, his director on *Sunset Boulevard* (1950), *Stalag 17* (1953), and *Sabrina* (1954), called him "the ideal motion-picture actor." Though a little old to play Hal—*Time* described the character as a young "sex bomb" who turns all the ladies' heads—thirty-seven-year-old Holden embodied the rough-hewn outsider in a way few of his peers could. As for Rosalind Russell, she viewed her part in *Picnic* as a strong comeback role. She appeared with little makeup, insisting the filmmakers not blot out her wrinkles. "I want to look like a real leathery Kansas dame," she declared.

The cast and crew traveled to the Sunflower State in the early summer of 1955 to capture an authentic look

Top: A moment of sibling rivalry, with Susan Strasberg, Kim Novak, and Betty Field
Middle: Kim Novak, Susan Strasberg, William Holden, and Cliff Robertson, changing after an afternoon swim
Bottom: Screen couple Rosalind Russell and Arthur O'Connell

and feel for the picture. Several Kansas towns were used, including Salina, Hutchinson, and Halstead, whose Riverside Park became the site of the picnic sequence. Joshua Logan was famous for his work on the stage, including *Annie Get Your Gun* (1946), *South Pacific* (1949), and the original *Picnic*, but had never before made a film—other than some uncredited reshoots for *Mister Roberts* (1955) at Warner Bros. In Kansas, he quickly became the dominant personality. As the *New York Times* reported during the shoot, "Logan is actor, writer, director, producer, photographer, sound engineer, prop man and every other technician on the set."

Logan was surrounded by Columbia's top creative talents, starting with screenwriter Daniel Taradash, who had recently won an Oscar for *From Here to Eternity* (1953). Costumes were made by legendary designer Jean Louis, dresser of Rita Hayworth, Marlene Dietrich, and others. Cinematographer James Wong Howe, who had worked in Hollywood since the silent era, captured the Kansas locations in vivid Technicolor and CinemaScope. The film's closing shot, taken by the young assistant camera operator Haskell Wexler, is an early example of aerial shooting via helicopter. Composer George Duning provides a score that sets the "mood of heated yearning" as one *Times* critic put it. The track "Moonglow and Theme from *Picnic*," a sultry fusion of the 1930s pop standard and original scoring, was used in the evening slow-dance sequence and later became a chart-topping hit.

Given the extent to which American culture has evolved since the Eisenhower era, audiences today might not fully grasp the impact such a sexually charged movie had at the time. As critic Roger Ebert noted during the film's 1996 restoration and theatrical rerelease, "It's hard to believe that *Picnic* was considered hot stuff in 1955. . . . It's a movie to show how attitudes have changed." And yet, more than just a time capsule, the film remains an evocative portrait of middle American life, its romantic hunger, and its summertime traditions.

Vacation Inspiration

William Inge's hometown of Independence, Kansas, is not only where you'll find his boyhood home and archives, but also the childhood home of *Little House on the Prairie* author Laura Ingalls Wilder. Since 1919 the annual Nee-wollah Festival (Halloween spelled backward) has taken place in October, the inspiration for the event in *Picnic*.

Make It a Double Feature

Splendor in the Grass (Warner Bros., 1961)

Another William Inge tale about a lovesick Kansas girl, this Elia Kazan–directed melodrama stars Natalie Wood in one of her most iconic roles. Warren Beatty costars as her handsome boyfriend, but her mother's warnings about "going too far" with boys lead to the couple's breakup—with disastrous consequences. Many elements from *Picnic* appear here as well, including a water motif in which its various forms—cascading falls, rushing rivers—symbolize sexual passion. Inge won an Academy Award for his original screenplay.

Warren Beatty and Natalie Wood

SMILES OF A SUMMER NIGHT

A group of unsatisfied lovers descend upon a country house for the summer solstice.

Director Ingmar Bergman ● **Producer** Allan Ekelund ● **Screenplay** Ingmar Bergman

Starring **Gunnar Björnstrand** Fredrik Egerman ● **Björn Bjelfvenstam** Henrik Egerman
Ulla Jacobsson Anne Egerman ● **Harriet Andersson** Petra ● **Eva Dahlbeck** Desiree Armfeldt
Margit Carlqvist Countess Charlotte Malcolm ● **Jarl Kulle** Count Carl-Magnus Malcolm
Naima Wifstrand Mrs. Armfeldt

Svensk
Filmindustri
(Sweden), 1955
B&W, 108 min.

American movies of the 1950s were in a period of transition. Their content, tone, and style were evolving to suit the tastes and concerns of a postwar world, and they were helped along by new waves of international cinema—in particular the thoughtful, artful, and free-spirited films of Ingmar Bergman. The first few of his movies to be released in the United States showed audiences what a special time summer is in Sweden, when the long winter finally gives way to warm weather, allowing people to escape their homes and live passionately together in nature.

The high-water mark of Bergman's early period is this summer farce, concerning the romantic entanglements of a man, his son, their maid, the man's current wife, his former lover, her current lover, his wife, and so on. The film is also a deeply trenchant and thoughtful evocation of love, loneliness, and belonging. Set at the turn of the twentieth century among upper and lower classes, its drama has as much to do with social status as it does libido. It takes place in the days leading up to Midsummer Eve, the shortest night of the year and the traditional kickoff of the summer holidays in Sweden.

The film begins with a few sets of poorly matched couples. The main character, a middle-aged lawyer named Fredrik Egerman (Gunnar Björnstrand), is in

◄◄ **Opposite page:** Petra (Harriet Andersson) and Anne (Ulla Jacobsson) share a lighthearted moment.

The original Swedish poster. *Smiles of a Summer Night* was later promoted in the United States as "a sexy frolic" starring Sweden's "most beautiful women."

his second marriage, still unconsummated, to nineteen-year-old Anne (Ulla Jacobsson). She is secretly in love with Fredrik's adult son, Henrik (Björn Bjelfvenstam), who is a devout theology student planning on a life in the priesthood. Their maid, Petra (Harriet Andersson), also has her eyes on young Henrik.

Meanwhile, Desiree Armfeldt (Eva Dahlbeck) is a stage actress who had an affair with Fredrik several years before, and the two become reunited when he seeks advice about his marriage. He flirts with Desiree, but she is currently in an affair with a married army officer, Count Carl-Magnus Malcolm (Jarl Kulle)—though she's secretly discontented.

All these lovers are brought together at the estate of Desiree's mother (Naima Wifstrand) for a dinner party on Midsummer Eve. Mrs. Armfeldt serves her guests a wine of "mysterious, stimulating power," which may or may not be the cause of everyone's subsequent dramatic interactions, reshuffling of affections, and general enlightenment. In the tradition of Shakespeare's comedy *A Midsummer Night's Dream*, a warm evening and a bit of magical influence rearrange an anxious group of lovers into more appropriate couplings.

The origins of Midsummer—called "the most typically Swedish tradition of all" and a de facto public holiday—lie in the feast day of John the Baptist, but it's also rooted in centuries of pagan ritual. Aligning with the summer solstice, Midsummer Eve is usually celebrated in the countryside with large gatherings, flower picking, maypole raising, dancing, drinking, games, and general revelry. It's also associated with fertility and the discovery of love. Legend has it that girls who place seven different flowers under their pillow will dream of their future husband.

Ingmar Bergman has a reputation for blending the sacred and the profane, and in this comedy he pits religious devotion and innocence against lust and adultery.

Top: The Countess (Margit Carlqvist) happily drinks the "stimulating" wine with Fredrik (Gunnar Björnstrand).
Middle: Henrik (Björn Bjelfvenstam) and Anne (Ulla Jacobsson) seem perfect for each other—but also terrible.
Bottom: Fredrik (Gunnar Björnstrand), Desiree (Eva Dahlbeck), and the Count (Jarl Kulle) form a love triangle—one of several.

His early films were marketed in the United States as kinky European divertissements and given racy titles: *Summer Interlude* (1951) became *Illicit Interlude*; *Summer with Monika* (1953) became *Monika: The Story of a Bad Girl*. American audiences would have found the Swedish summer to be quite exotic, with its long nights and general "feeling of freedom," says Harriet Andersson, who played the lead role in *Summer with Monika*. "Even now . . . you can still find a place where you can be your own Harry and Monika, and run around nude. . . . It's stupid to put on a bathing suit. Just go into the water and dry in the sun."

Smiles of a Summer Night won acclaim for Bergman in Europe, including a special prize at the 1956 Cannes Film Festival, and it opened new doors for the director. His next movie, *The Seventh Seal* (1957), would be the beginning of a new chapter of artistic and commercial success. An existential drama, it famously depicts a returning Crusader (Max Von Sydow), who plays a game of chess with the black-robed figure of Death on a rocky beach. It was the breakout hit for Bergman internationally, playing in art house theaters in the United States for many months and leading to a wider interest in, and critical reevaluation of, his earlier films.

In 1961, famously mercurial film critic Pauline Kael called *Smiles of a Summer Night* "a nearly perfect work" and an "exquisite carnal comedy." Noting that Bergman

Petra (Harriet Andersson) finds happiness with felow servant Frid (Åke Fridell).

had directed a stage adaptation of *The Merry Widow* just before, which influenced his decision to set the film at the turn of the century, she writes, "The film is bathed in beauty, removed from the banalities of short skirts and modern-day streets and shops, and, removed in time, it draws us *closer*."

Bergman worked in a steady pattern, making a film each summer while directing live theater and opera through the colder months. Many of his films include an overt reference to the theater, including the actress character Desiree Armfeldt and the traveling troupe of performers in *The Seventh Seal*. Fittingly, *Smiles of a Summer Night* was itself later adapted into a popular stage production, Steven Sondheim's *A Little Night Music* (1973), which contains the famous ballad "Send in the Clowns," sung by Desiree in a moment of vulnerability.

Mrs. Armfeldt (Naima Wifstrand) hosts a Midsummer Eve dinner for the mismatched lovers.

Vacation Inspiration

Summer is the best time to visit Sweden, when warm weather sends its residents into the countryside to enjoy the many beautiful forests, lakes, and rivers. You can also visit Bergman's home on the island of Fårö, where the director worked for over forty years.

A Midsummer Night's Dream (Warner Bros., 1935)

Shakespeare's fantastical comedy about a group of lovers, an acting troupe, and fairies who wreak havoc in the forest one night was given a lavish treatment by Warner Bros., which turned the reins over to theater impresario Max Reinhardt. With lush, Oscar-winning cinematography (the only write-in winner in Academy history), the film's production values and sheer scale remain impressive, as does the cast: James Cagney, Mickey Rooney, Dick Powell, and Olivia de Havilland in her first screen role.

James Cagney and Joe E. Brown

GIDGET

A teenage girl takes up surfing—and love—while in the company of Malibu beach bums.

Director Paul Wendkos ● **Producer** Lewis J. Rachmil ● **Screenplay** Gabrielle Upton, based on the novel *Gidget: The Little Girl with Big Ideas* by Frederick Kohner

Starring **Sandra Dee** Frances Lawrence (Gidget) ● **James Darren** Jeffrey Matthews (Moondoggie) ● **Cliff Robertson** Burt Vail (The Big Kahuna) ● **Arthur O'Connell** Russell Lawrence ● **Mary LaRoche** Dorothy Lawrence ● **Joby Baker** Stinky ● **Tom Laughlin** Lover Boy ● **Sue George** Betty Louise (B. L.)

Columbia, 1959
Color, 95 min.

At the age of fifteen, young Kathy Kohner headed to Malibu to ingratiate herself with the local surfers, hoping to catch a wave herself. A few years later, her father—a Hollywood screenwriter who had emigrated from Austria before World War II—published a novel based on her diaries, naming the main character Gidget, a portmanteau of "girl" and "midget." The book in turn inspired this classic 1959 film, which turned his daughter into a major figure in the surfing world and ushered in a wave of beach-set movies plus a couple of sequels, a 1965 television series with Sally Field, and even stage adaptations.

The charming thing about Gidget (whose real name is Frances Lawrence) is her all-American gee-whiz wholesomeness. She gets along just swell with her parents, is a straight-A student, and even plays the cello. Noting her one area of deficiency, a friend remarks, "The kid's studied up on about everything but sex." Gidget is sixteen, but she doesn't quite fit in with her more well-developed and worldly peers, who at the beginning of summer whisk her off to the beach to go "manhunting."

While her girlfriends are there solely to attract the attention of boys—even sending a beach ball flying accidentally-on-purpose in their direction—Gidget would rather just be having fun in the water. "Honey, maybe you need a few hormone shots," one friend says. Gidget shrugs and puts on her snorkel gear.

As it turns out, the boys are heading out into the ocean, too, surfboards in tow. When Gidget gets tangled in some kelp, she is rescued by young Moondoggie (James Darren), who surfs her back to shore, where she meets the other guys. That one ride is all it takes to get her excited about surfing, and soon she begs her father to buy her a board. From that point on, her summer is dedicated to catching waves.

Her girlfriends put her down as a tomboy. More accurately, she's just a spirited girl who isn't interested in the narrow gender role epitomized by her peer group. It's fair to say that she's not yet comfortable owning her sexuality, but she can be just as feminine as the rest of them, as she proves during her impromptu date with Moondoggie. Gidget feels comfortable among the guys and being an active participant with them, not the object of their gaze. What does motivate her, and what

Advertisements played up the film's romantic aspects while reminding viewers of Kohner's hit novel.

◄ **Opposite page:** A moody Moondoggie (James Darren) stands between Gidget (Sandra Dee) and Kahuna (Cliff Robertson).

Gidget (Sandra Dee) with her beloved surfboard

she finds truly thrilling, is surfing. She does her best to describe the ecstasy she feels: "It was like nothing I ever felt before! Whoop! We're on an elevator headed for the sky. And then, zoom! Speeding across the ocean, on top of the world!"

Even outside the film world, it has been suggested that you can divide the history of surfing into two categories—pre-*Gidget* and post-*Gidget*—because of the movie's revolutionary impact. Along with the pioneering surf movies of director Bud Browne—beginning with *Hawaiian Surfing Movie* (1953)—*Gidget* led to the development of an entirely new genre: the beach movie. In the sporting world, surfing had remained relatively obscure during the 1950s, a hobby for those outside the mainstream—and it certainly wasn't for girls. Case in point: in the film's surfing sequences, her rides are performed by a male stuntman in a woman's bathing suit. "Surfing's not for dames!" taunt the beach bums. But the

one-two punch of Kohner's book and Columbia's film changed the sport forever.

Gidget's parents (Arthur O'Connell and Mary LaRoche) are excited that she's interested in an outdoor sport—they even make a surfing-themed cake for her seventeenth birthday—but they're naturally cautious as they watch their "little girl" grow up. At one point her mother reminds Gidget of a family motto: "To be a real woman is to bring out the best in a man." The film, still a studio product of the 1950s, tries to have its cake and eat it, too.

Columbia was hoping for a hit when it picked up the film rights to Kohner's novel. The studio poured resources into the production, shooting on location in Malibu, in CinemaScope and vivid color by award-winning cinematographer Burnett Guffey. The producers inserted a few musical sequences, including a performance by the male quartet the Four Preps (who also

Gidget explains the thrill of surfing to her parents (Mary LaRoche and Arthur O'Connell).

Gidget and her surfer friends Kahuna (Cliff Robertson), Lord Byron (Burt Metcalfe), Waikiki
(Doug McClure), Lover Boy (Tom Laughlin), Hot Shot (Robert Ellis), and Stinky (Joby Baker) below

Sandra Dee and Cliff Robertson at the luau

sing the title track) and a couple of songs from Darren, who became a recording artist and teen idol thanks to the film. Columbia star Cliff Robertson plays the Big Kahuna, a Korean War veteran turned beach bum, and sort of elder statesman of the surfing gang. He stands apart from the others, not just because of his age and experience, but also because of his dedication to a life outside the mainstream, free of societal restrictions. "For them, it's a summer romance," he explains to Gidget. "For me, it's a full-time passion."

Sandra Dee's star was on the rise in 1959, when she also appeared in *Imitation of Life*, which became

Universal's biggest box-office hit up to that time, and *A Summer Place* at Warner Bros. Dee was under contract to Universal, who had loaned her to Columbia for *Gidget* but wouldn't let her participate in the theatrical sequels. *Gidget Goes Hawaiian* (1961) instead starred Deborah Walley; *Gidget Goes to Rome* (1963) featured Cindy Carol. Still, the good-girl persona would follow her for the rest of her life, even being satirized in the song "Look at Me, I'm Sandra Dee" in the 1971 musical *Grease*.

As for Kathy Kohner, she inspired a generation of young women athletes with what has been called "girl power" of the 1950s, wrapped up in a wholesome, all-American package. Now Kathy Kohner-Zuckerman, she was recently named one of the sport's most influential figures by *Surfer* magazine—a publication that was founded in the wake of *Gidget*—whose editor Sam George said the movie "marked one of the most definitive epochs in surfing history. After that, everyone suddenly was looking at surfing."

Vacation Inspiration

Malibu's Leo Carrillo State Park was the primary location for the film's beach scenes. But there are many such photogenic locations in Malibu, which stretches for twenty-one miles along the Pacific coast, west of Los Angeles. You may not find the crowds typical of other beaches in Southern California, but plenty of surfers will be out riding the waves.

A Summer Place (Warner Bros., 1959)

Sandra Dee made this soapy melodrama with costar Troy Donahue just after *Gidget*. It tells of two former lovers (Richard Egan and Dorothy Maguire) who reunite, only to discover that their children by previous marriages are falling in love, too. A landmark depiction of teenage summer love, the film is set on the East Coast but was filmed in California, with Monterey standing in for Maine, a secret that is given away when the sun sets over the ocean. One piece of the film's incredible scenery is the Clinton Walker House in Carmel, designed by Frank Lloyd Wright, which becomes the parents' beach home.

Sandra Dee and Troy Donahue

THE PARENT TRAP

When long lost twin sisters meet at summer camp, they decide to fool their parents and switch places.

Director David Swift ● **Producer** Walt Disney ● **Screenplay** David Swift, based on the book *Das doppelte Lottchen* by Erich Kästner

Starring **Hayley Mills** Susan Evers / Sharon McKendrick
Maureen O'Hara Maggie McKendrick ● **Brian Keith** Mitch Evers
Joanna Barnes Vicky Robinson ● **Charlie Ruggles** Charles McKendrick
Una Merkel Verbena ● **Leo G. Carroll** Rev. Dr. Mosby

Buena Vista,
1961
Color, 129 min.

Summer camp isn't always a life-changing experience, but with a little Disney magic it becomes a setting for self-realization (in addition to canoeing, hiking, and awkward coed dances). Starring Hayley Mills as two twin sisters, separated as infants and raised on opposite sides of the country, the film is a mix of summer fantasy, coming-of-age story, and—when the girls scheme to get their divorced parents back together—a comedy of remarriage. It's also good clean fun, the kind for which Walt Disney has always been known.

Short-haired Susan Evers lives in California with her dad, Mitch (Brian Keith); long-haired Sharon McKendrick lives in Boston with her mother, Maggie (Maureen O'Hara). There's clearly a family resemblance between the blonde and blue-eyed girls. When Sharon arrives at Camp Inch by chauffeur—bringing both a high society accent and a book of poetry—one of Susan's friends declares, "The nerve of her, coming here with your face!" Another jokes, "I'd bite off her nose. Then she wouldn't look like you."

What starts as annoyance quickly turns to animosity. A canoe gets overturned, a cabin gets muddied and soiled, and Susan is humiliated when the back of her dress is surreptitiously cut away. When things turn physical at the dance, complete with a large cake landing on the face of the camp director, Miss Inch (Ruth

McDevitt), Sharon and Susan are put together in an isolation cabin away from the others for the remainder of camp. Miss Inch tells them, "Either you'll find a way to live with each other or you'll punish yourselves far better than I ever could."

Her plan works. The cabin, aptly named "Serendipity," is where the girls finally realize that

The Parent Trap was written and directed by David Swift, a former Disney animator and television writer who had adapted *Pollyanna* (1960) for the screen.

they're indeed sisters. Eager to see each other's parents, they hatch a plan to swap identities, live as each other for a time, and ultimately lure their parents back together. "Sooner or later they'd have to unswitch us . . . and they'd have to meet again."

That plan works, too. But what first follows are some genuinely emotional scenes between the girls and their long-absent parents. For instance, when Susan reunites with her mother for the first time in years, it's an undeniably touching moment played to perfection by O'Hara. "Did you miss me?" her mother asks. Susan—as Sharon—replies, "You'll never know."

The story had been adapted from the 1949 German book *Das doppelte Lottchen* by Erich Kästner (published as *Lottie and Lisa* in the United States), based on an idea the author had pitched as a movie scenario during the war. It became popular the world over and has spawned many films since its release, starting with the West German production *Two Times Lotte* (1950). That was followed by the Japanese film *The Lullaby of Hibari* (1951) and the British *Twice Upon a Time* (1953), the only solo directing credit of Emeric Pressburger. Among the many versions since *The Parent Trap* was released, the most famous may be the 1998 remake written and

Top: Sharon and Susan perform "Let's Get Together," which had been the film's working title.
Middle: Sharon and Susan come to terms at "Serendipity," their isolation cabin.
Bottom: Brian Keith and Maureen O'Hara also starred together in Sam Peckinpah's directorial debut, *The Deadly Companions* (1961), which premiered the same month as *The Parent Trap*.

Camp Inch is fictional, but *The Parent Trap* was shot in the San Bernardino Mountains in the area around Lake Arrowhead and Big Bear Valley. This part of California is definitely worth a visit, as is the coastal town of Carmel, the setting for the film's second act.

directed by Nancy Meyers, starring a young Lindsay Lohan as both sisters. "It's a very girl-empowering movie," Meyers says, recalling her love for the original film. "The two girls make everything happen. They have total control of the destiny of their family."

The plot device of two sisters separated in infancy and unaware of each other until meeting at the same summer camp is certainly dramatically compelling (even if it strains credibility in the real world). But it presented certain challenges for filmmakers: first, to make sure the two girls were identifiable and distinct; second, to actually film identical twins together on screen, with both characters being played by Mills. Part of the responsibility lay with writer-director David Swift, who crafted a carefully plotted screenplay accounting for each girl's background, preoccupations, and personality. But the film's believability with audiences also required some technical wizardry.

The results are a testament to the showmanship and expert filmmaking chops at Walt Disney Productions. The special effects are designed to be invisible and all in service to the story, and even watching the film today with CGI-jaded eyes, we fully believe we're seeing two girls interacting on screen together. In addition to shots using body doubles and split-screen effects, the filmmakers were able to capture both characters' faces in the same shot using a sodium vapor process to create high-quality traveling mattes. Also known as yellowscreen, this compositing technology was developed in the previous decade by engineer Petro Vlahos and used extensively by Disney because it achieved better results than the more common bluescreen method of the era. This kind of cutting-edge technology put the studio at the forefront of special effects work in the 1960s.

Of course, none of this would have mattered without Hayley Mills, whom Walt Disney called "the greatest movie find in twenty-five years." The daughter of actor John Mills and writer Mary Hayley Bell (author of the 1959 novel *Whistle Down the Wind*), she appeared in six films for Disney, beginning with *Pollyanna* (1960), which won her an honorary Juvenile Academy Award. She received the miniature Oscar two months before the

Maureen O'Hara and Brian Keith, with Leo G. Carroll (center), one of Alfred Hitchcock's most utilized character actors

hard not to be charmed by her intelligent and affecting performance, made all the more impressive by her difficult double role.

The 1960s were a decade of huge changes in the American film industry, as producers and studio executives chased an ever-evolving audience. Disney was the only major studio making movies for kids in the early 1960s, with Mills as its brightest star, but it was positioned at the end of one era and the beginning of another. Domestic upheaval and influences from abroad, mostly from European filmmakers, would expand the conversation about what film can be and what it should represent. Filmmakers themselves would get younger and more experimental. The language of film would alter, as would the content; the end of the Production Code would lead to more mature themes and depictions on screen.

premiere of *The Parent Trap*, which would be her most successful film at the studio. She even had a popular hit with the film's song "Let's Get Together," which was written by the Sherman Brothers (in their first film for Disney) and reached number eight on the US charts. It's

Luckily for us, the spirit of summer remains largely the same. Stories of life at camp continue to be made, because getting out into nature—whether through the lens of Ingmar Bergman, or Walt Disney, or Wes Anderson—remains an essential summer tradition.

Three Smart Girls (Universal, 1936)

Young actress-singer Deanna Durbin made a name for herself in this hit musical comedy. Durbin costars with Nan Grey and Barbara Read, who play three sisters who try to stop their divorced father (Charles Winninger) from getting remarried to a gold-digging socialite (Binnie Barnes)—and instead reunite with their mother (Nella Walker). The movie's box-office success saved Universal from bankruptcy, and Durbin became the studio's most bankable star (she was nicknamed "the mortgage lifter"). *Three Smart Girls* remains a charming family comedy and—with its girl-powered plot—a clear forerunner to *The Parent Trap*.

Barbara Read, Deanna Durbin, and Nan Grey

THE MUSIC MAN

A traveling salesman attempts to dupe an Iowa town and seduce the local librarian.

Director Morton DaCosta ⬤ **Producer** Morton DaCosta ⬤ **Screenplay** Marion Hargrove, based on the play by Meredith Willson, in collaboration with Franklin Lacey

Starring **Robert Preston** Harold Hill ⬤ **Shirley Jones** Marian Paroo
Buddy Hackett Marcellus Washburn ⬤ **Hermione Gingold** Eulalie Mackechnie Shinn
Paul Ford Mayor George Shinn ⬤ **Pert Kelton** Mrs. Paroo ⬤ **Ron Howard** Winthrop Paroo
Timmy Everett Tommy Djilas ⬤ **Susan Luckey** Zaneeta Shinn

Warner Bros., 1962 Color, 151 min.

Few musicals bring to mind flag-waving Americana like Meredith Willson's *The Music Man*—partly because of its small town, turn-of-the-century setting, and partly because it begins on a sunny Independence Day and has a thing or two to say about America's political proclivities.

Harold Hill (Robert Preston) is a traveling salesman whose specialty is selling folks a dream and then skipping town. In this case, he tells the good people of River City, Iowa, that he can help save the young men of the town from iniquity by channeling their energies into something positive: a marching band. This being middle America, Harold exploits the patriotic fervor of the Fourth of July celebration to stoke their excitement, convince them of his musical expertise, and start collecting cash for instruments, uniforms, and instruction books.

His fellow salesmen complain, "He's a fake, and he doesn't know the territory!" Well, he'll come to know the territory soon enough. It turns out that Iowa has a reputation for stubbornness, so selling his schtick there may not be so easy. But Harold is up for the challenge. Hopping off the train, he asks a local, "What do you folks do around here for excitement?" The stern man replies, "Mind our business."

An old friend and accomplice, Marcellus Washburn (Buddy Hackett), gives him the lay of the land and

Top: Shirley Jones and Robert Preston. *The Music Man* was nominated for six Academy Awards, including Best Picture.
Bottom: Shirley Jones and Pert Kelton, outside on a warm Iowa evening.

warns him in particular about the town's shrewd librarian (Shirley Jones): "She'll expose you before you get this bag unpacked." Harold jokes, "I'll back her into a corner and breathe on her glasses." Little does he know how bewitching he will find her: Marian the librarian, the only person in town not taken in by the charlatan.

◄◄ Opposite page: Robert Preston gets all the kids excited.

Top: The mayor's wife (Hermione Gingold, at left) and a brood of gossipy townswomen
Bottom: Marian the librarian isn't taken in by "Professor" Harold Hill.

One of the many catchy songs that made the stage show a landmark of American musical theater is "Ya Got Trouble," which introduces Harold to the townspeople and explains how a fast-talking, confident huckster can rile up a group of citizens ripe for the picking. He appeals to their fears with a ridiculous argument connecting the local billiard parlor to the downfall of their city. "Folks, ya got trouble—right here in River City—with a capital 'T' and that rhymes with 'P' and that stands for Pool!" Preston's performance here is electric and makes us believe how Hill could make a career out of these sorts of elaborate schemes—he's a born salesman.

Emboldened, he tries to thread the needle by asking out Marian at the Fourth of July fireworks. Sure enough, she's skeptical. When he refers to himself as Professor Hill, she's indignant. "Professor? Of what?" she asks. "At what college do they give a degree for accosting women like a Saturday night rowdy at a public dance hall?" Only over time is he able to disarm her, in part through sheer tenacity. All the local men ignore her, thinking she's a know-it-all.

It becomes clear that there's a connection between the two characters, and not just a romantic one. Marian, who's a piano teacher in addition to her job in the library, is the perfect foil for "music man" Harold Hill, who can't tell one note from another. Tellingly, her yearning ballad "Goodnight, My Someone" is written with the same chord structure as his rousing march "Seventy-Six Trombones," suggesting that the two characters are actually more in sync than they may at first seem.

We can still see the dichotomy represented by the librarian and the salesman in the America of today: the poised intellectual versus the populist rabble-rouser. Marian is stuffy and studious, relying on facts and expertise, and is open to diverse ideas and cultures. In one scene, she defends a book of classical Persian poetry to the mayor's wife, who suspects it to be "smutty" material. Harold is outgoing and chummy but appeals to the town's basic fears in order to swindle them out of their money. He ill-advises Marian's young brother, Winthrop (Ron Howard), "Never allow the demands of tomorrow to interfere with the pleasures and excitements of today."

And yet, Harold also seems to bring out the best in River City. Four members of the school board, who have "hated each other for fifteen years," are told by Harold that they harmonize wonderfully (they actually do, since they're performed by a real barbershop quartet, the Buffalo Bills). Soon they're inseparable. Meanwhile little Winthrop, embarrassed by his lisp, finally comes out of his shell when Harold promises him a cornet and a place in the band. The whole town seems happier and more hopeful.

What is the film saying about middle America? It's certainly a cautionary tale, a warning to be wary of men selling hopes and dreams with elusive credentials, but it also celebrates the warmth of small-town life and the

Though the film was shot on the Warner Bros. lot in Burbank (the Santa Monica Mountains are visible in one scene), you can visit Music Man Square and see Meredith Willson's boyhood home, now a museum, in Mason City, Iowa. It's also where the movie had its premiere in 1962.

Harold Hill arrives just in time for Independence Day.

aspirations of average people who just want their kids to be happy . . . and maybe throw a big parade. It's enough to warm the heart of even cynical Harold Hill.

The music reflects this attitude, and the breeziness of many of the songs (like "The Wells Fargo Wagon") captures the cheerful optimism of the time and place. It also matches the film's character types, such as Harold's verbose sing-talk style ("Singing is just sustained talking,"

he says) and Marian's "Piano Lesson," in which her vocal line arpeggiates along with a practicing piano student. Songs are also written with mimicry and satire, like the salesmen's opening number that adopts the pulsating rhythm of the train, and the townswomen's song "Pick-a-Little, Talk-a-Little," which suggests they're a brood of hens.

Credit for the great songwriting goes to composer Meredith Willson, an Iowan by birth and a flautist who had played with John Philip Sousa's band in the 1920s. He had previously worked in Hollywood as a film composer, earning Oscar nominations for the scores to *The Great Dictator* (1940) and *The Little Foxes* (1941). One of his most famous songs was "It's Beginning to Look a Lot Like Christmas," recorded by Perry Como and the Fontane Sisters in 1951. But he will always be most closely associated with *The Music Man* and its irresistible depiction of Midwest America in the summertime.

Nashville (Paramount, 1975)

Here is another summery musical of sorts, this time depicting the colorful residents (and dreamers) of the Tennessee capital, the epicenter of country music. Lurking throughout is political candidate Hal Philip Walker of the "Replacement Party," whose campaign van drives around the city broadcasting pseudo-patriotic nonsense, and whose gala concert brings all the musical acts together at the end of the movie. Director Robert Altman masterfully satirizes both politics and the music industry, while also applauding individuals who have the guts to pursue their dreams, even when it seems futile.

Lily Tomlin

THE ENDLESS SUMMER

Two young surfers travel around the world in search of the perfect wave.

Director Bruce Brown ● **Producer** Robert Bagley and Bruce Brown
Screenplay Bruce Brown

Starring **Mike Hynson** Principal Surfer ● **Robert August** Principal Surfer
Bruce Brown Narrator

Bruce Brown
Films, 1964
Color, 95 min.

Few activities evoke "fun in the sun" quite like surfing, and Bruce Brown's celebrated film is the archetypal documentary of the sport. It was a labor of love for the Southern Californian filmmaker, who grew up surfing, joined the Navy after high school, and was stationed in Hawaii, where he began taking 8mm movies of his adventures. Brown raised $50,000 to make *The Endless Summer*, shooting, editing, and even narrating the film himself. Distributors were skeptical, but after touring with the film and a successful year-long booking in a New York theater, it became clear that audiences were hungry for something so carefree and undeniably cinematic.

Described by the *New York Times* as the "Fellini of the foam," Brown set an aesthetic tone for the many surfing documentaries that followed. Full of long takes of guys shooting the waves, it's punctuated by some silly comedic moments and layered with Brown's laid-back commentary—informative, but informal—and a buoyant soundtrack by the '60s band the Sandals. If the film has a villain, it's mother nature, whose inconsistency keep the heroes traveling the globe in search of the perfect wave. Otherwise it can be enjoyed like a relaxing day at the beach. Just chill out and soak in the view.

"Summer means many different things to different people," the film's narration begins. "To some, it might mean the thrill of a high-speed catamaran. Others like

← **Opposite page:** Robert August and Mike Hynson spend time among the natives.

The Endless Summer

On any day of the year it's summer somewhere in the world. Bruce Brown's latest color film highlights the adventures of two young American surfers, Robert August and Mike Hynson who follow this everlasting summer a-round the world. Their unique expedition takes them to Senegal, Ghana, Nigeria, South Africa, Australia, New Zealand, Tahiti, Hawaii and California. Share their experiences as they search the world for that perfect wave which may be forming just over the next Horizon. **BRUCE BROWN FILMS**

Filmmaker Bruce Brown began screening *The Endless Summer* for audiences in 1964. Two years later, it was picked up by arthouse distributor Cinema V.

to float around and soak up a few stray rays. Still others like some kind of inland activity. But for us, it's the sport of surfing!" Much of the opening section was shot in California and introduces various surfing styles and terminology ("staying in the curl"; "riding the nose"), as well as a few of the area's major figures: Lance Carson, Miki Dora, and others. The film also explains what a

wipeout is and shows several examples. In surfing, even failure looks like fun.

While the surf gets bigger in California in the wintertime, the water is quite cold. Brown explains that surfers ride in all seasons, but "the ultimate thing for most of us would be to have an endless summer: the warm water and waves without the summer crowds of California." Accepting this challenge, Brown decides to accompany two surfers, Robert August and Mike Hynson, on a trip around the world to chase the summer season. Brown shows a humorous scene of them preparing for West Africa: they study books titled "Shark Attack: Field Dressings Illustrated" and "Malaria Manual" and then

Top: Director Bruce Brown with Robert August
Bottom: Mike Hynson heads out.

pack a suitcase full of nothing but swim trunks, board wax, a portable radio, and a single band-aid ("in case of injury"). They leave Los Angeles on a cloudy November day and head for Dakar, Senegal.

So begins an adventurous travelogue in which two fish-out-of-water American boys experience new cultures while introducing the local population to some culture of their own: we're told no Africans had surfed here before. In surfer lingo, getting a feel for the water is "getting the place wired." Once Mike and Robert are familiarized with the current, the music shifts from an exotic, tribal beat back to the Sandals' jaunty beach-rock score.

They next head to Ghana, where their only drama is how to travel by car with a surfboard, and on to Nigeria with its water temperature a steamy 91 degrees. The attitude is good-natured throughout, but the narration is a product of its time. It refers to the Africans as "natives" who "may never have seen a white man before," ignoring their recent history as British colonies. Brown jokes of Ghana, "The only English word they knew was 'Hang Ten.'"

Arriving next in Cape Town, South Africa, where it's truly summer in November, they're excited to meet more "natives": the young girls who hang out on the beach. Then on to Australia, New Zealand, Tahiti, and Hawaii. The film's holy grail is the "perfect wave," explained as a small wave with a perfect shape. Brown says the odds

Shooting the curl

against finding one are "ten million to one." A dubious statistic, maybe, but who cares?

In the late 1950s, Bruce Brown had been recruited by Venice Beach boardmaker Dale Velzy to film his surf team and help promote the sport. With $5,000, he got a camera, a book on how to make movies, and flew with the surfers to Hawaii. The result was *Slippery When Wet* (1958), which Brown would narrate live at the film's screenings. He then spent several years making low-budget surfing films. In 1962 he compiled his best footage into the anthology *Water Logged* ("90 exciting minutes of surfriding thrills"), in order to raise the money for his biggest production to date, *The Endless Summer*.

The unburdened spirit of the film—Do these guys have jobs or responsibilities?—is a reflection of its limited resources and thus freedom of production. Bruce

Mike Hynson and Robert August pack light.

Vacation Inspiration

Hawaii is surfing's spiritual home. You can start with some beginner lessons at Waikiki Beach, before taking a drive up to Oahu's North Shore, where you'll find the world's best surfers riding some incredible waves at Waimea Bay and the famed Banzai Pipeline.

Brown answered to no one; *The Endless Summer* was made outside studio interference, without regard for Hollywood's established rules of filmmaking, and it has since become one of the most iconic films ever made. Brown's narration isn't that of the traditional documentarian: it represents the point of view of a surfer, rather than an observer. He's not studying surfing so much as letting the audience in on his hobby.

Of course, any documentary on this subject—or fiction film, for that matter—is at an advantage. "Surfing seems almost impossible to ruin on the big screen," writes Elvis Mitchell of the *New York Times*. "It's so photogenic that it's hard to believe that color film wasn't invented just to capture it." From *Gidget* (1959), to *Ride the Wild Surf* (1964), to *Point Break* (1991), film dramas have channeled the excitement of surfing for decades. Brown himself continued filming the sport, making *The Endless Summer II* in 1994 with his son Dana, who later carried on the family tradition with the documentary *Step into Liquid* (2003).

Make It a Double Feature

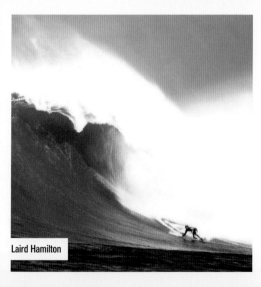

Laird Hamilton

Riding Giants (Sony Pictures Classics, 2004) This gripping documentary traces the history of surfing from its Polynesian roots to present-day big wave riders, explaining its evolution from countercultural lifestyle to mainstream appeal. It also features interviews with notable surfers like Greg Noll, famous for his feats at Oahu's Waimea Bay in the 1950s, and Laird Hamilton, who helped develop tow-in surfing in the 1990s, which revolutionized the sport and allowed for ever-bigger and more dangerous rides.

BEACH BLANKET BINGO

A party of bikini-clad teenagers is disrupted by the arrival of a new pop singer.

Director William Asher ● **Producers** Samuel Z. Arkoff and James H. Nicholson
Screenplay William Asher and Leo Townsend

Starring **Frankie Avalon** Frankie ● **Annette Funicello** Dee Dee
Jody McCrea Bonehead ● **Paul Lynde** Bullets ● **Linda Evans** Sugar Kane
John Ashley Steve ● **Deborah Walley** Bonnie ● **Harvey Lembeck** Eric Von Zipper
Don Rickles Big Drop ● **Buster Keaton** Buster

American International Pictures, 1965 Color, 98 min.

As the fifth and arguably best entry in a beach party series from American International Pictures, *Beach Blanket Bingo* is the epitome of a lighthearted summer movie. Like the lives of its young characters, it's a loosely structured frolic in the sand and surf of Southern California featuring doe-eyed love, groovy rock 'n' roll, winking sexual vibes, goofy comedy gags, and lots of bikinis and tanned torsos. None of it should be taken too seriously. As one surfer dude says, "It's a wiggy beach."

Between 1946 and 1960 the number of teenagers in America more than doubled, and Hollywood was taking notice. Suddenly the swinging '60s were here, and Baby Boomers were calling the shots. This movie reflects a free and easy attitude expressed by the postwar generation, with a playful tone and the occasional break into song.

Naturally, the movie opens on the beach, where the characters live together in a cozy bungalow. Like *Gidget* (1959), it was filmed at Leo Carrillo State Park in Malibu, but now middle-class teenagers have overrun the surfer bums. Frankie (Frankie Avalon) and Dee Dee (Annette Funicello) tune their portable radio to something upbeat, landing on the song "Beach Blanket Bingo." Cue the opening credits, as the whole crowd begins to twist on the sand. "Take a blanket made for

two now / Add a boy and a girl / That's the game for me and you now / Yeah let's give it a whirl!"

To kick off the story, a young female skydiver descends into their sunny paradise. When several young guys paddle out to rescue her from the water, they discover that she's the beautiful pop singer Sugar Kane (Linda Evans), and the dive was an elaborate publicity

The BEACH PARTY gang goes SKY DIVING!

BEACH BLANKET BINGO

AN AMERICAN INTERNATIONAL PICTURE
in COLOR and PANAVISION®

STARRING

FRANKIE AVALON · ANNETTE FUNICELLO · DEBORAH WALLEY · HARVEY LEMBECK
JOHN ASHLEY · JODY McCREA · DONNA LOREN · MARTA KRISTEN · LINDA EVANS
BOBBI SHAW · DON RICKLES · PAUL LYNDE | BUSTER KEATON · EARL WILSON
as "BIG DROP"   as "BULLETS"

written by WILLIAM ASHER & LEO TOWNSEND directed by WILLIAM ASHER produced by JAMES H. NICHOLSON & SAMUEL Z. ARKOFF co-producer ANTHONY CARRAS

◄◄ **Opposite page:** Frankie Avalon, Annette Funicello, Deborah Walley, and John Ashley

Beach Blanket Bingo was the fifth film in a series that began with *Beach Party* (1963) and ended with *The Ghost in the Invisible Bikini* (1966).

Top: The beach party films contain some of Buster Keaton's final screen performances.
Bottom: Frankie Avalon and Annette Funicello costarred in almost all of AIP's beach party films.

stunt by her crafty agent, Bullets (Paul Lynde). He giddily envisions the headline "Singer Saved by Surfers," and he's brought along New York gossip columnist Earl Wilson (appearing as himself) to cover the event. Sugar Kane strips off her diving suit to reveal a candy-striped bikini. The kids are wise to the publicist's scheme, but the guys are nonetheless attracted to the singer, calling her a "groovy chick."

All this excitement causes Frankie and several others to want to try out skydiving themselves. The next day they visit Big Drop's skydiving center (run by Don Rickles) to learn the ropes. Meanwhile, their dopey friend Bonehead (Jody McCrea) stays behind to do some surfing on his own. When he wipes out, he finds himself rescued by a mysterious woman—in fact, a mermaid named Lorelai (Marta Kristen). When Sugar runs out from the beach to help, Lorelai swims off to avoid detection. Predictably, the publicist turns the episode into a story of Sugar coming to a surfer's rescue. "Just rest your head back in Sugar's lap, boy," he instructs Bonehead, snapping a photo.

One of the film's main themes is the exploitation of youth culture by patronizing businessmen. Bullets has a keen sense of what the kids want, and he positions his product—Sugar's new record—to take full advantage of their appetite for sex and pop music. Ironically, this is exactly the strategy of the film's studio, American International Pictures (AIP), an independent production

In addition to surfing, summer is the perfect time to experience other thrills just as the characters in *Beach Blanket Bingo* do. These days, you can try out skydiving outdoors or indoors, or maybe opt for a more serene parasail ride over the beach.

and distribution company whose films were designed specifically for a teenage audience. Its first release was *The Fast and the Furious* (1954), a low-budget crime movie produced by Roger Corman, who would go on to make many films with AIP.

"To the big studios, the youth culture was an unknown entity," founder Sam Arkoff recalled. "But I could see who was going to the movies, and it was young people." AIP chose to give their films a clear anti-establishment

Annette Funicello and Frankie Avalon watch Sugar Kane skydive over the ocean, with Donna Michelle, Mike Nader, Patti Chandler, and Jody McCrea.

angle, rather than what Arkoff believed the major studios were selling teenagers: "a moral lesson, a lecture . . . By the late '50s the kids were beyond lecturing." To get things just right, AIP would first develop colorful titles and brief plot outlines, which they would submit to teenage focus groups to gauge interest. Their movies were a direct result of the feedback they received. All this explains why the beach party series includes adult characters who are phony and manipulative; only the kids have integrity, and they're also out to have a good time.

Full of little trick shots, playful editing, comedic gags, and musical sequences, *Beach Blanket Bingo* often plays more like one of the era's TV variety shows rather than a typical narrative film, as when Don Rickles does a quick stand-up routine before introducing the movie's surf-rock band, the Hondells, who perform with Sugar Kane. Much of the plot is straightforward and can be boiled down to simple "will they / won't they" romantic conflicts, like that of Frankie and Dee Dee. But it's taken to an almost wistful level with the subplot of Bonehead falling in love with a mermaid.

Bonehead (Jody McCrea) gets plenty of human attention, but falls for a mermaid instead.

Things get downright goofy when the local biker gang shows up. Their leader is Eric Von Zipper (Harvey Lembeck), a leather-clad, Harley-riding meathead who takes a liking to Sugar Kane but calls the surfers "undesirables." Broad comic relief is provided by silent film star Buster Keaton, who, while fishing during the opening sequence, casts his line and accidentally hooks a girl's bikini top, sending it flying out to sea.

Even potentially serious moments are treated satirically. Inside the beach house, Donna Loren roasts a hot dog in the fireplace while singing the ballad "It Only Hurts When I Cry." A young man is seen with tears streaming down his face, but the camera later pans down to reveal that he's slicing onions. By the time she has finished singing, her hot dog has burned to a crisp.

AIP ultimately made seven beach party films from 1963 to 1966, as well as a few spinoffs like *Ski Party* (1965) and *Sergeant Deadhead* (1965). Other studios got in on the act, too, with films such as Fox's *Surf Party* (1964) and Paramount's *The Girls on the Beach* (1965).

Of the recurring cast members at AIP, perhaps the most indicative of the new teen generation in the early 1960s was Annette Funicello, an original Disney Mouseketeer who had become famous for her wholesome roles and charming voice. When Walt Disney asked Arkoff, "What are you doing to my little girl?" he replied, "We're just letting her be her age."

Make It a Double Feature

Blue Hawaii (Paramount, 1961)

Elvis Presley was in his heyday as a movie star in the early 1960s, and this tropical musical is one of his most iconic. Made a year after Presley was discharged from the US Army, it tells of a soldier who returns home to Hawaii to surf, sing, and reconnect with his girlfriend (Joan Blackman). Disenchanted with the family pineapple business, he opts instead to become a Honolulu tour guide and is soon leading (and leading on) a group of young women around the islands. Filmed extensively on Oahu and Kauai, the film includes many memorable tunes, including the title track—which had debuted decades earlier in *Waikiki Wedding* (1937)—and the new ballad "Can't Help Falling in Love."

Joan Blackman and Elvis Presley

THE GRADUATE

A disaffected college graduate has a summer affair with an older family friend.

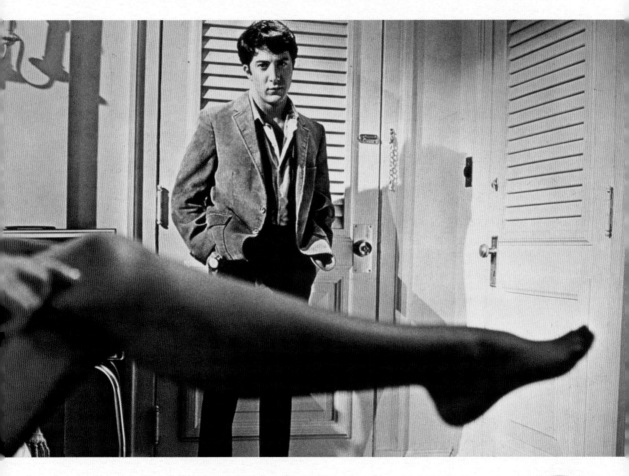

Director Mike Nichols ● **Producer** Lawrence Turman ● **Screenplay** Buck Henry and Calder Willingham, based on the novel by Charles Webb

Starring **Dustin Hoffman** Benjamin Braddock ● **Anne Bancroft** Mrs. Robinson
Katharine Ross Elaine Robinson ● **William Daniels** Mr. Braddock
Elizabeth Wilson Mrs. Braddock ● **Murray Hamilton** Mr. Robinson

Embassy Pictures, 1967 Color, 106 min.

Benjamin Braddock (Dustin Hoffman) is a pitiable character despite having every traditional social advantage. He is a college track star and recent graduate who, perhaps because of the expectations thrust upon him by his parents and society, feels unsure of how to move on with his life. His quiet awkwardness and antisocial tendencies aren't the stuff of the traditional movie hero, but *The Graduate* is a movie so beloved that it has come to stand for a whole generation of young people who looked skeptically upon the world they were handed in the late 1960s.

Benjamin is the subject of many now-iconic moments, two of which involve being caught in the frame with Mrs. Robinson's (Anne Bancroft's) leg in the foreground. The film opens with him riding a moving walkway at the airport, where he is pulled along to his destination like a piece of luggage. He bangs his fists on a church window at the end of film, in a mix of fury and desperation. He is often pictured against water: sitting in front of an aquarium in his bedroom or wearing a scuba diving suit at the bottom of his pool. It's fair to say Ben is metaphorically adrift, or maybe drowning. Film critic Jamie Bernard suggests he "feels nothing as he floats in the amniotic fluid of that summer of indecision between college and real life."

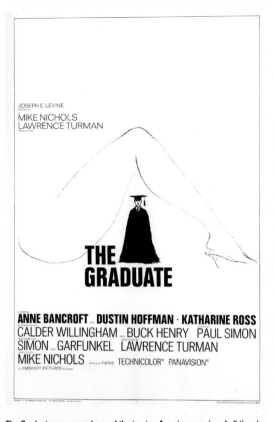

JOSEPH E. LEVINE PRESENTS
MIKE NICHOLS
LAWRENCE TURMAN PRODUCTION

THE GRADUATE

STARRING ANNE BANCROFT AS MRS DUSTIN HOFFMAN · KATHARINE ROSS
SCREENPLAY BY CALDER WILLINGHAM AND BUCK HENRY MUSIC BY PAUL SIMON
SIMON AND GARFUNKEL PRODUCED BY LAWRENCE TURMAN
MIKE NICHOLS PRINTS BY PATHE TECHNICOLOR® PANAVISION®
AN EMBASSY PICTURES RELEASE

The Graduate was named one of the top ten American movies of all time by the American Film Institute in 1998.

It's in his scuba suit—a birthday present from his parents, who grab his mask and push him below the surface—that he makes his decision to call Mrs. Robinson. We witness their first meeting in the Taft Hotel, where Benjamin keeps the bedroom poorly lit out of an abundance of caution. It reads like a noir, with light coming in through slanted window blinds and curling cigarette smoke—and Mrs. Robinson as the femme fatale.

◀◀ **Opposite page:** Recent graduate Benjamin Braddock (Dustin Hoffman) finds Mrs. Robinson very compelling.

Top: Katharine Ross and Dustin Hoffman escape together.
Bottom: Anne Bancroft was thirty-five during filming, just six years older than Dustin Hoffman.

Minutes later, we see Benjamin back at the swimming pool, but this time he's floating serenely on a raft, bare-chested and tanned, without a care in the world. He's finally above water, comfortable, and in control. Even if he's not sure where all this is leading.

Ben's summer is played out in an elaborate montage. He hops from the pool to the hotel room with Mrs. Robinson, back to the pool, and so on. The music of Simon and Garfunkel narrates the calendar of emotions, with a reprise of the lonely anthem "The Sound of Silence" and the story of a brief summer romance, "April Come She Will," which foretells the end of the affair: "The autumn winds blow chilly and cold / A love once new has now grown old."

The film's soundtrack is legendary, its songs probably even more well-known than the movie, although only one was written specifically for the film—"Mrs. Robinson"—which appears in a simplified format, without the full set of lyrics that would later be heard on its 1968 single. The elegiac "Scarborough Fair/Canticle" is used in the film's second half, as Ben is trying to get his life in order.

"Ben, what are you doing?" his father (William Daniels) asks. "Look, I think it's a very good thing that a young man, after he's done some very good work, should have a chance to relax and enjoy himself and lie around and drink beer and so on. But after a few weeks, I believe that person would want to take some stock in

Top: With their affair on the skids, Ben (Dustin Hoffman) asks Mrs. Robinson (Anne Bancroft), "Do you think we could liven it up with a little conversation for a change?" **Bottom:** Mike Nichols and cinematographer Robert Surtees (in cap) film Dustin Hoffman in the pool.

himself and his situation and start to think about getting off his ass!" Ben has had a lazy summer, living in a sort of dream, but now he decides to take action. After an awkward date with Mrs. Robinson's daughter, Elaine (Katharine Ross), Ben decides to pursue her, following her back to school at Berkeley that fall.

The Graduate has long been understood in popular culture to be a story of youthful rebellion, about a new generation not accepting the world of their parents. This is borne out in the choices Ben makes, as he seems to do the opposite of what his elders want from him. He begins an affair that would shock his parents, then resists their urging him to date Elaine, then later takes Elaine out in defiance of Mrs. Robinson's stern prohibition. He'll continue rebelling until the very end of the movie. It seems he can please no one, so he may as well please himself.

Ben's story originated in the novel *The Graduate*, written by Charles Webb and published in 1963. It sold only a few thousand copies and wouldn't be a bestseller

Benjamin in his birthday present

until the film generated reinterest. Two writers took a stab at a screenplay. Calder Willingham is credited with

Vacation Inspiration

Reenact Ben's drive to Berkeley with a road trip to the Bay Area. Though most of the film was shot around Los Angeles, including the campuses of USC and UCLA, Ben is seen driving across the Oakland Bay Bridge (albeit in the wrong direction), visiting the San Francisco Zoo, and spying on Elaine in Berkeley's Sproul Plaza.

having written an early, unused draft, but Buck Henry—who appears as the hotel clerk who asks Benjamin if he's there "for an affair"—wrote the final script, much of which is taken verbatim from Webb's text.

It turns out the late 1960s was a perfect time for the movie, as a new generation of filmmakers was given license by the studios to tell daring new stories for a grown-up audience. *The Graduate* has all the hallmarks of the "New Hollywood" era: formal inventiveness, youthful disaffection, mature content. Director Mike Nichols, coming off his successful debut film, *Who's Afraid of Virginia Woolf?* (1966), lent a fresh eye to the production. He brought on veteran cinematographer Robert Surtees, who used telephoto and zoom lenses to great effect, and Broadway costume designer Patricia Zipprodt, who dressed Mrs. Robinson in a series of suggestive animal prints.

The film's final scene has been much debated. Where do the characters go from here? Will they find happiness? It's entirely possible that Ben may never be totally satisfied with life, always chasing the peace he felt while floating in the pool on a hot summer afternoon.

Make It a Double Feature

Ghost World (United Artists, 2001)

High school graduates Enid (Thora Birch) and Rebecca (Scarlett Johansson) are just as aimless as Benjamin Braddock, but much more cynical about their suburban world. The two best friends plan to get jobs and live together, but Enid is told she needs one more credit to receive her diploma. While taking an art class that summer, she meets the older, vintage-blues-loving Seymour (Steve Buscemi) and forms an unexpected bond. Director Terry Zwigoff's Oscar-nominated film was adapted from the graphic novel by Daniel Clowes and has become a cult classic.

Scarlett Johansson and Thora Birch

JAWS

A giant shark terrorizes beachgoers one summer in New England.

Director Steven Spielberg ⬤ **Producers** David Brown and Richard D. Zanuck
Screenplay Peter Benchley and Carl Gottlieb, based on the book by Benchley

**Universal, 1975
Color, 124 min.**

Starring **Roy Scheider** Chief Martin Brody ⬤ **Richard Dreyfuss** Matt Hooper
Robert Shaw Quint ⬤ **Lorraine Gary** Ellen Brody ⬤ **Murray Hamilton** Mayor Vaughn
Carl Gottlieb Meadows ⬤ **Jeffrey Kramer** Deputy Hendricks ⬤ **Susan Backlinie** Chrissie

S teven Spielberg's terrifying *Jaws* is the iconic summer thriller, "as unavoidable a staple of summer as heat and humidity," according to critic Molly Haskell. Set around the Fourth of July in the picturesque seaside resort of Amity Island, the film imagines a world in which the American ideal—a warm, sunny, middle-class utopia—is beset with lurking danger.

The main character, Martin Brody (Roy Scheider), has just moved with his wife, Ellen (Lorraine Gary), and son (Chris Rebello) from New York to be the police chief of what he expects to be a quiet and laid-back town. Indeed, nothing too bad generally seems to happen on Amity Island, which thrives on vacationers each summer. So when a fatal shark attack is reported one morning and Brody suggests closing the beach, he is met with opposition from incredulous locals, Mayor Vaughn (Murray Hamilton) in particular. "Amity is a summer town. We need summer dollars," the mayor stresses. "If people can't swim here, they'll be glad to swim at the beaches at Cape Cod, the Hamptons, Long Island." Brody relents and things continue as normal, with holiday-goers flocking to the beach.

The first attack had occurred at night upon a lone swimmer—a young woman skinny dipping—and could be written off as some sort of divine punishment for living recklessly, as so often seems to happen in horror

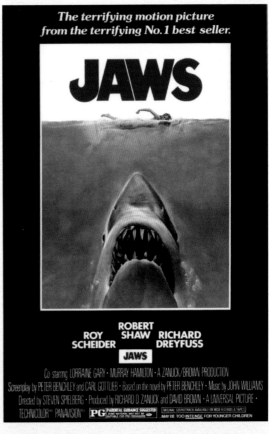

Jaws was a monster of a movie, the first to earn $100 million at the box office.

movies. But soon the shark is attacking indiscriminately—kids!—during an otherwise pleasant afternoon. The carnage is not only an assault on the characters, it's a blow against the very idea of a fun day at the beach. Some terrified moviegoers never went back into the water after seeing *Jaws*; many more still eye the ocean suspiciously. According to its screenwriter Carl Gottlieb, *Jaws* did

◄◄ **Opposite page:** Roy Scheider as Chief Brody

Top: Robert Shaw as veteran shark hunter Quint
Bottom: Richard Dreyfuss as oceanographer Matt Hooper

for the ocean what *Psycho* (1960) had done for the shower, affecting a generation with a fear of open water.

The film was based on the debut novel by Peter Benchley, who appears in the film as a TV interviewer. He originally had low expectations for his book "about a fish," but producers Richard D. Zanuck and David Brown purchased the film rights before the novel had even been published, and they hired Benchley to write the first draft of the screenplay. The film was released

at a time of national anxiety, only a few months after the close of the Vietnam War and less than a year after Watergate had forced the resignation of Richard Nixon. It's no coincidence that it depicts a Fourth of July in which the island's residents are nervous and fearful of an unseen threat.

Jaws definitely struck a chord with audiences, quickly becoming the biggest movie hit of all time and the first to reach $100 million at the domestic box office. Released in June 1975, it helped launch a new breed of film known as the summer blockbuster, relying on a huge advertising campaign to open widely on its first weekend. The person most credited with its success has been director Steven Spielberg, who up to that point had made only a few smaller-budgeted movies, including *The Sugarland Express* (1974) with producers Zanuck and Brown. His film *Duel* (1971), made for Universal but released as an ABC "Movie of the Week," had featured a menacing truck that Spielberg considered to be a forerunner to the shark in *Jaws*.

The cast was led by Roy Scheider, who had coincidentally appeared as a New York police detective in *The French Connection* (1971), and a young Richard Dreyfuss, star of the popular film *American Graffiti* (1973). The grizzled shark hunter, Quint, is played by English actor Robert Shaw, famous for films such as *From Russia with Love* (1963) and *A Man for All Seasons* (1966). Quint's monologue about the sinking of

One of several animatronic sharks used for the film

Jaws was shot on the beautiful island of Martha's Vineyard, a summer beach resort easily accessible by ferry from Cape Cod. Check into a bed-and-breakfast, grab a bicycle, and explore the backroads, lighthouses, and picturesque cottages of this New England jewel.

the USS *Indianapolis*—a true event, in which stranded crewmen were slowly picked off by sharks—is a mesmerizing moment of dread before the film's gripping final act. Quint is essentially a Captain Ahab figure, fixated on squaring off with the creature that haunts his memories.

For the shark itself, Spielberg employed several full-sized animatronic great whites, with the goal of filming them in the actual ocean. A team of engineers led by Robert Mattey—the technical wizard behind the giant squid and submarine for Disney's *20,000 Leagues Under the Sea* (1954)—built right- and left-profile versions, but

they proved very difficult to operate in open water and led to constant delays in shooting. Fixing the animatronics would have required some downtime, but David Brown worried that a pause in filming would have given the studio an excuse to shut down production altogether—"If you take the film out of the camera, they might not let you put it back in"—so they pressed on.

An even bigger concern was the believability of the hulking mechanical shark, which Spielberg had now nicknamed "Bruce," after his lawyer. To help ensure that it would invoke fright instead of laughter, Spielberg avoided putting the shark on screen for much of the film's running time and carefully staged its entrances so that the shock of seeing it would override any problems the audience might have with its appearance.

Spielberg also turned to gifted composer John Williams, who created an unorthodox musical score that has transcended even the film itself. Notably simplistic, its rhythmic, thumping bass notes—like the heartbeat of a monster—suggest an unstoppable force charging

The shark's first victim (Susan Backlinie). The color red was reserved almost exclusively for blood in *Jaws*, to make scenes of violence more shocking.

ahead to its next victim. It is used masterfully in the film: the audience is conditioned to expect the shark's arrival when the music is heard; and conversely, Spielberg can withhold the music, making the audience jump when the shark suddenly appears out of the silence. Without its indelible score, Spielberg says, the film would have only been "half as successful."

Left: Robert Shaw, Roy Scheider, and Richard Dreyfuss need a bigger boat.

Make It a Double Feature

Blue Water, White Death

(National General Pictures, 1971)

This landmark documentary about great white sharks, reportedly the inspiration for Peter Benchley's novel, features the Australian diving team—married couple Ron and Valerie Taylor—that Spielberg later hired to film the cage diving sequences in *Jaws*. Director and photographer Peter Gimbel leads a crew across the Indian Ocean in search of the predator, capturing some groundbreaking underwater sequences. The *New York Times* declared that it has "some of the most smashing, man-against-beast footage ever filmed by anyone anywhere at any time."

BREAKING AWAY

Four aimless Indiana high school graduates challenge the local university in an epic bicycle race.

Director Peter Yates ● **Producer** Peter Yates ● **Screenplay** Steve Tesich

Starring **Dennis Christopher** Dave Stohler ● **Dennis Quaid** Mike

Daniel Stern Cyril ● **Jackie Earle Haley** Moocher ● **Barbara Barrie** Mom

Paul Dooley Dad ● **Robyn Douglass** Katherine ● **Hart Bochner** Rod

Twentieth Century-Fox, 1979 Color, 101 min.

n this beloved sports movie, four scrawny midwestern boys take an extended summer vacation. All are recent high school graduates, but none has moved beyond the proverbial "summer after graduation," when life's big decisions start to be made. When we meet them, they're out of work and don't know what to do with their lives.

Part of the problem is economic. They're lower-class kids, known to locals as "cutters"—short for stonecutters, a reference to the region's declining blue-collar industry—but they're stuck in the college town of Bloomington and find themselves at odds with the Indiana University students who have bright futures and drive expensive cars. For cutters, good jobs are scarce. Main character Dave Stohler (Dennis Christopher), whose father (Paul Dooley) runs a used-car dealership, uses a bike as his main mode of transportation, and it has become his passion.

The film's title is both literal ("breaking away" from the pack, in cycling terminology) and metaphorical: Dave and his friends need to escape from the hold their hometown has on them and begin their adult lives. They were born cutters, and they can't seem to lose the stereotype.

Breaking Away is full of sweaty bike rides and afternoon swimming trips at the local quarry. Presumably the film tracks the boys over the course of a full academic

◀◀ **Opposite page:** Dave (Dennis Christopher) races through his pain at the Little 500.

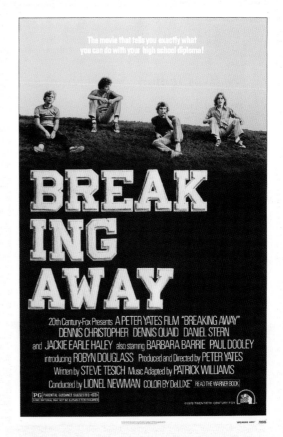

Steve Tesich's screenplay was lauded by the New York Film Critics Circle, the National Society of Film Critics, the Writers Guild of America, and the Academy.

year—the cycling event featured in the film, the Little 500, is held each year in April—but we never see evidence of an Indiana winter. Instead, the film seems to exist in a permanent summer, just as the characters do.

The boys are in a rebellious solidarity; to become productive members of society would violate their unwritten pact. "All for one and one for all," says handsome Mike (Dennis Quaid), who was recently fired from the A&P grocery. He had been a successful high school football quarterback, and he stays in shape in the hopes of someday playing again. Diminutive Moocher (Jackie Earle Haley) gets a job at a gas station but quits when the boss calls him "shorty." Tall and lanky Cyril (Daniel Stern) was a basketball player who didn't get the scholarship he expected. "I kinda miss school, ya know?" he says in the opening scene. "I mean, this is gonna be the first time no one's gonna ask us to write a theme about how we spent our summer."

Dave is the serious cyclist of the group, and after winning a Masi bicycle he's become obsessed with Italian culture. He sings a famous piece from *La Traviata* while riding through his neighborhood streets, shouting "Ciao, bambini!" at the local kids. He wears Neapolitan Sunset cologne and calls his pet cat "Fellini." When he learns that an Italian cycling team is coming to Bloomington for a race, he's thrilled to be able to compete alongside them. He even adopts an Italian persona to win the affections of an IU student, Kathy (Robyn Douglass). She drops a notebook on the sidewalk one day as she's riding off on her Vespa—surely an auspicious sign—and Dave returns it to her, pretending to be an exchange student named Enrico.

Dave's father—a no-nonsense, meat-and-potatoes type—is frustrated with Dave's hobby and lack of job prospects. "He's never tired! He's never miserable!

Top: Dave in his element
Middle: An abandoned limestone quarry is now the boys' favorite swimming hole.
Bottom: Paul Dooley as Dave's dad, owner of a used-car dealership

When I was young, I was tired and miserable!" He is shocked to find Dave shaving his legs (to gain speed on the bike) and rails against his Italian fixation. When he suggests Dave could work as a stonecutter, like he had after high school, his wife (Barbara Barrie) points out that most of the quarries have closed.

Dave's mom is supportive and even joins in the cultural appreciation, putting on an opera record one night to seduce her husband. It's a sweet moment, intercut with a scene in which Dave—as Enrico—serenades Kathy outside her sorority house.

When the friends get into a brawl with some students on campus, the university administration is inspired to allow a town team to compete in the upcoming Little 500, to let their discord play out in a healthy arena. The boys sign up for the fifty-mile relay—under the assumption that Dave can bike the whole thing himself—and proudly call themselves the "Cutters."

Breaking Away romanticizes cycling and reveals it to be inherently cinematic, with its simultaneous speed and grace. The film's "speed test" sequence, in which Dave

Dave poses as Italian student "Enrico" to impress Katherine (Robyn Douglass).

races down a highway behind a semitrailer, is thrilling in the way that the famous car chase in director Peter Yates's earlier film *Bullitt* (1968) was. The semitrailer truck is especially meaningful for Dave, as it's branded Cinzano, the Italian vermouth brand that sponsors the film's visiting racing team. He is clearly at home on his bike, whether coasting along a wooded road or zipping

Vacation Inspiration

Be like Dave and take a road bike tour of Bloomington, Indiana. Most of the film's locations are still standing, with the notable exception of the Tenth Street Stadium, site of the film's Little 500 race. Held each April, the "World's Greatest College Weekend" now also includes a women's Little 500.

Dave (Dennis Christopher) and his dad (Paul Dooley), who is taken aback by his son's love for all things Italian.

down the highway, and all the riding sequences are scored to classical music—including Rossini's *The Barber of Seville* and Mendelssohn's *Italian Symphony*—playing for the audience what Dave is likely hearing in his head.

The film launched the careers of several of its young actors. It represented the first major screen roles of Christopher, Quaid, and Stern; Haley was the young-est of the four and had previously played supporting parts in several high-profile films, like *The Bad News Bears* (1976). First-time screenwriter Steve Tesich was an alumnus of IU and had ridden in the Little 500 as a student in 1962. He based the character of Dave on his teammate, Dave Blase, who appears on screen as a race announcer. The film was shot in and around

Bloomington and also includes a cameo by IU's then president, John Ryan.

With a cast of unknowns and a small budget, the film was an underdog, and it relied on the support of film critics to help find its footing with audiences. It became an unlikely box-office hit and has remained popular ever since, even being named one of the top ten sports films of all time by the American Film Institute in 2008.

Right: The Cutters: Dennis Christopher, Jackie Earle Haley, Daniel Stern, and Dennis Quaid

Make It a Double Feature

Chariots of Fire (Warner Bros., 1981)

Another rousing sports movie from the era of *Breaking Away* (with Dennis Christopher in a minor role), this inspirational tale of British athletes at the 1924 Summer Olympics won the hearts of an international audience—and a surprise Best Picture trophy at the Academy Awards. Ian Charleson stars as morally conflicted runner and Christian missionary Eric Liddell, with Ben Cross as his Jewish teammate Harold Abrahams. Another small-scale film that became a crowd pleaser, it's perhaps best known today for its much-imitated beach sequence and electronic musical score by Vangelis.

Ian Charleson and fellow Olympians

CADDYSHACK

A young man spends his summer as a golf caddie to earn money for college.

Director Harold Ramis ● **Producer** Douglas Kenney ● **Screenplay** Brian Doyle-Murray, Douglas Kenney, and Harold Ramis

Starring **Michael O'Keefe** Danny Noonan ● **Chevy Chase** Ty Webb
Ted Knight Judge Elihu Smails ● **Bill Murray** Carl Spackler
Rodney Dangerfield Al Czervik ● **Cindy Morgan** Lacey Underall
Scott Colomby Tony D'Annunzio ● **Sarah Holcomb** Maggie O'Hooligan
Dan Resin Dr. Beeper ● **Henry Wilcoxon** Bishop Fred Pickering

**Warner Bros.,
1980
Color, 98 min.**

This 1980s cult classic and preeminent golf comedy, chock-full of memorable characters and quotable lines ("Be the Ball"), is also a great movie about a summer job. Like other young suburban kids with no hard skills, Danny Noonan (Michael O'Keefe) turns to manual labor to earn money for college. He becomes a golf caddie at the prestigious Bushwood Country Club, where he can get face time with rich members, earn tips, and forge some lucrative relationships. He's a pretty good player, too, and proves his worth in both a caddie tournament and a high-stakes game during the film's finale. And that's about as serious as this movie gets.

Though Danny is the main character, his story isn't what has made Caddyshack a staple of pop culture. At its heart, Harold Ramis's comedy is as much about goofballs as golf balls, a showcase for some of the funniest actors of the era, including Chevy Chase and his Saturday Night Live successor, Bill Murray. What began as a coming-of-age film devolved during production into a series of hilarious gags. Large portions of the film were improvised, like Murray's famous "Cinderella story" monologue in which he fantasizes about winning the Masters tournament while lopping off the heads of a row of chrysanthemums.

When it was released in July of 1980, the film was only modestly successful. Reviews were largely lukewarm; some were scathing. The *Hollywood Reporter* wrote, "To attempt a critical evaluation of Orion's new *Caddyshack* is a little like describing the aesthetic qualities of an outhouse." The *Washington Post* called it "a derelict farce." Unlike the megahit *National Lampoon's Animal House* (1978), for which Ramis cowrote the screenplay, it took years for *Caddyshack* to find a wide

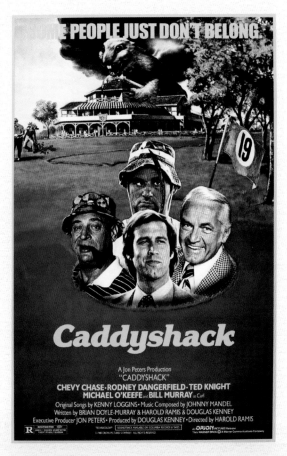

Though Michael O'Keefe's Danny is ostensibly the film's main character, he was overshadowed by its other stars.

◄◄ **Opposite page:** Bill Murray and the troublesome gopher

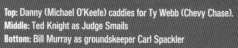

Top: Danny (Michael O'Keefe) caddies for Ty Webb (Chevy Chase).
Middle: Ted Knight as Judge Smails
Bottom: Bill Murray as groundskeeper Carl Spackler

Chevy Chase as Ty Webb

and appreciative audience. But as Chris Nashawaty has written in his book-length survey of the film, "It was *Caddyshack*'s imperfections that ended up making it so perfect."

At the beginning of the film, Danny caddies for Ty Webb (Chase), with whom he discusses his future. "I gotta go to college," Danny says. "I'm gonna end up working in the lumber yard the rest of my life." Webb replies that he owns two lumber yards, but he's "not sure where they are." The movie foregrounds class difference, contrasting the stuffy clubhouse with the humble and rowdy caddyshack. It also pokes fun at some of the club's wealthy idiots—including the cantankerous, Rolls-Royce-driving owner, Judge Elihu Smails (Ted Knight), and his nemesis, the wisecracking eccentric Al Czervik (Rodney Dangerfield), whose golf bag is complete with a telephone and beer tap. "The man's a

menace!" yells the Judge, who later hurls his putter in a fit of rage and accidently strikes a club member.

Meanwhile a pesky gopher is menacing the golf course, tunneling down fairways and ripping up greens. Smails is furious, and oddball groundskeeper Carl Spackler (Murray) is instructed to "kill every gopher on the course." Carl spends the rest of the film attempting to exterminate the rodent, to ridiculous ends. He also gives the film's most memorable ramblings, including a story about the time he caddied for the Dalai Lama, who, in lieu of a tip, promised him "total consciousness" on his deathbed. "So, I got that goin' for me," he says, "which is nice."

The film is full of absurd moments like this. During a violent rainstorm, Carl caddies for Bishop Pickering (veteran actor Henry Wilcoxon), who shoots the best round of his life before being struck by lightning on the eighteenth green. There are also famous bits of sophomoric humor, like the swimming pool's Baby Ruth scene, complete with a *Jaws*-like musical cue. During the club's Fourth of July banquet, Czervik lets out a conspicuous fart at the dining table and quips, "Somebody step on a duck?"

Chalk up the film's loose style to the party-like atmosphere on set, which was by all accounts alcohol-soaked and drug-fueled. O'Keefe later remarked that if you remember making *Caddyshack*, "you probably weren't there." Though set in Nebraska, the film's

Visit some of the film's South Florida locations, like Key Biscayne, the site of the film's yacht club sequence. Or simply spend the day at your local country club. Just be sure to tip your caddie.

winter shooting schedule dictated a move to South Florida. Filming took place mainly at Rolling Hills Golf & Tennis Club in Davie (now Grande Oaks Country Club), which was chosen in part because it didn't have any visible palm trees. The finale's pyrotechnics—in which Carl sets off a series of explosions to root out the gopher—were apparently reported to the nearby Fort Lauderdale airport by a concerned pilot.

Producer and cowriter Doug Kenney had been a cofounder of *National Lampoon* magazine in 1969 and had helped write *Animal House*, while Ramis, Chase, Murray, and cowriter Brian Doyle-Murray (Bill's brother, who appears as Lou Loomis, the caddyshack's manager) had all been a part of the magazine and its associated stage and radio shows. The story of an upwardly mobile teenager who works as a summer caddie had been inspired by the experiences of the Murrays and their four other brothers, who had all caddied in their youth in Winnetka, Illinois, and who were inducted into the Caddie Hall of Fame in 2015.

Judge Smails (Ted Knight) and his nemesis, Al Czervik (Rodney Dangerfield)

Other notable contributions to the film come from Kenny Loggins, who wrote several of the songs, including opening and closing credits track "I'm Alright," and John Dykstra, the head special effects artist on *Star Wars* (1977), who created the gopher puppet that famously dances to Loggins's music. It's this kind of silliness that makes the film such a great diversion. *Caddyshack* is a low-stakes movie full of lowbrow humor, perfect for a lazy summer day.

The Caddy (Paramount, 1953)

Dean Martin and Jerry Lewis made over a dozen movies together, including this story of a talented golfer (Lewis) who gets too nervous playing in competition and decides instead to caddie for Martin's character. Because of their hilarious chemistry, the pair eventually get scooped up by a theatrical producer and turned into a stage act. The film features Lewis's trademark goofiness and some smooth crooning from Martin, including the classic tune "That's Amore." Look out for cameos from several famous golfers, including Ben Hogan, Sam Snead, and Byron Nelson.

Donna Reed, Jerry Lewis, and Dean Martin

ON GOLDEN POND

An elderly couple spend the summer at their lake house with an unexpected teenage visitor.

Director Mark Rydell ● **Producer** Bruce Gilbert ● **Screenplay** Ernest Thompson, based on his play

Starring **Henry Fonda** Norman Thayer ● **Katharine Hepburn** Ethel Thayer
Jane Fonda Chelsea Thayer ● **Doug McKeon** Billy Ray ● **Dabney Coleman** Bill Ray
William Lanteau Charlie

Universal, 1981
Color, 109 min.

W riter Ernest Thompson has said his play *On Golden Pond* is about "the end of an era" in which Americans would spend their entire summer—from the end of the school year to Labor Day—at the lake. "It was paradise," he nostalgizes. In the film adaptation, we witness this tradition through the eyes of a long-married couple, Norman (Henry Fonda) and Ethel (Katharine Hepburn), who have been coming to their lake house every summer for decades. Not only a place of retreat where one can experience the quiet pleasures of nature, Golden Pond represents to Norman and Ethel all the years gone by and the life they have forged together.

Norman will soon be turning eighty and feels increasingly out of touch with the world. The film is about his many relationships—marital, fatherly, intergenerational—and the process of reconciliation we see on screen between Norman and his daughter, Chelsea (Jane Fonda), was also playing out behind the camera. Jane Fonda had purchased the rights to Thompson's play so that her father could star in the film, the message of which is forgiveness and understanding—made all the more poignant by the easing of the real-life relatives' famously strained relationship.

The story is predictable; we know exactly where it's going before it gets there. But that doesn't detract from the movie's pleasures, which include heartfelt

On Golden Pond won Oscars for Henry Fonda and Katharine Hepburn, as well as its screenplay.

performances from all involved. Katharine Hepburn and Henry Fonda play a believably married couple who each seem to know what the other is thinking without having to speak. Jane Fonda plays a complex and emotionally frayed daughter without ever veering into melodrama. Though unabashedly sentimental, the screenplay

◄◄ **Opposite page:** Henry Fonda and Katharine Hepburn enjoying the lake

is intelligent and has great respect for the multifaceted lives of its characters.

The loons, noisy with their wails and tremolos, are a summer staple at Golden Pond. Ethel, hale and hearty in her late sixties, cheerfully welcomes them when they arrive at the lake house early in the film. Norman, a retired professor, has slowed down considerably and sees reminders of his mortality everywhere; he plays them off with sarcasm and morbid humor. When he notes that the cottage has termites, which he suggests is "not such a bad way to go," Ethel remarks, "Your fascination with dying is beginning to frazzle my good humor." In one notable scene, she sends him into the forest to pick strawberries, but Norman returns empty-handed, having gotten suddenly disoriented and scared without her nearby. "You're my knight in shining armor," she reassures him. "You're going to get back on that horse and I'm gonna be right there behind you, holding on tight, and away we're gonna go, go, go."

Conflict arises when Chelsea brings her new boyfriend, Bill (Dabney Coleman), and his teenage son, Billy (Doug McKeon), to Golden Pond, suggesting that Billy can stay with her parents while she and Bill vacation in Europe together. The thirteen-year-old, dismayed and intimidated, starts out by trying to appear tough.

Top: "Life marches by, Chels," advises Ethel (Katharine Hepburn). "I suggest you get on with it."
Middle: Billy (Doug McKeon), Chelsea (Jane Fonda), and Norman (Henry Fonda)
Bottom: The family reunites for Norman's eightieth birthday.

He precociously says that he and his friends "cruise for chicks" in their spare time. But Norman soon gets him to lower his defenses, asking him if he likes the word "bullshit," since he uses it so often. When Billy says yes, Norman nods. "It's a good word." Feeling more comfortable, Billy decides to go fishing with them. "I thought I might come along," he says, arriving at the dock, "and see what this bullshit is all about." They welcome him aboard their boat and Norman surprises him by how fast it can go. Soon Billy is practicing backflips off a floating diving board while Norman serves as his coach. Their friendship is mutually beneficial: Billy gains maturity and self-confidence, while Norman's spirit grows younger and less curmudgeonly.

One of the movie's themes is the divide between city and country. Director Mark Rydell describes Chelsea's boyfriend, Bill, as a "city boy" from Los Angeles who doesn't feel comfortable at the lake. At one point he nervously asks Ethel about a mysterious shape in the forest. "That's a lawn chair," she replies. She and Norman are perfectly at ease in the great outdoors, as is Chelsea, right back where she spent her childhood summers. "I

Henry Fonda and Katharine Hepburn, in their first movie together

don't think I've ever grown up on Golden Pond," she confides to her mother. "I act like a big person everywhere else."

To Rydell's credit, the film doesn't try to sugarcoat its characters. Norman is crotchety and rude, and often creates uncomfortable situations. Consider the scene in which Bill asks for permission for him and Chelsea to sleep in the same bed. Rather than getting visibly upset, Norman toys with Bill, asking with a straight face if he might be more comfortable "abusing my daughter" on the hearth? When Bill accuses him of antagonizing

Vacation Inspiration

Outdoorsy New Hampshire makes a fine getaway during the hot summer months. You can rent a cottage on Squam Lake or nearby Lake Winnipesaukee and take a tour of the film's locations from the town of Holderness.

Jane Fonda goes for a swim.

him, Norman says, "Let's get back to talking about sex. Anything you want to know, just ask me."

Henry Fonda performs with sharp-eyed intelligence. His acting partner, the warbly voiced Hepburn, gives one of the sweetest and most selfless performances of her career. It's also very physical, as when she dives off the front of a boat to come to Norman's rescue, late in the film. In a deleted scene, she even picks up and carries a canoe down to the lake by herself. The golden-age stars, who had never met before filming began, would both win Academy Awards for their performances.

On Golden Pond was shot at Squam Lake in New Hampshire. Because it was surrounded by private homes, Mark Rydell had to appear before the local board to seek their approval before filming began. He shrewdly brought Hepburn along. According to the director, the town was so "overwhelmed by her presence that they quickly gave us permission to shoot there." It seems many people were taken by Hepburn—and the film in general. It grossed over $100 million domestically and became the second biggest movie of 1981, behind Raiders of the Lost Ark.

Make It a Double Feature

Two for the Road
(Twentieth Century-Fox, 1967)

Stanley Donen's romantic comedy follows a married couple (Albert Finney and Audrey Hepburn) who reflect on earlier road trips they have taken to the south of France. Their newfound affluence—Finney plays a successful architect—is contrasted with earlier years when they were poorer but happy, hitchhiking and scrounging up makeshift dinners. It's a charming and bittersweet look at an evolving marriage that has faced its share of challenges, all depicted through a series of lovely summer vacations.

Albert Finney and Audrey Hepburn

NATIONAL LAMPOON'S VACATION

A hopelessly optimistic father takes his family on an epic road trip to their favorite California theme park.

Director Harold Ramis ◉ **Producer** Matty Simmons ◉ **Screenplay** John Hughes, based on his short story "Vacation '58"

Starring **Chevy Chase** Clark W. Griswold ◉ **Beverly D'Angelo** Ellen Griswold **Anthony Michael Hall** Rusty Griswold ◉ **Dana Barron** Audrey Griswold **Randy Quaid** Cousin Eddie ◉ **Miriam Flynn** Cousin Catherine ◉ **Imogene Coca** Aunt Edna **Christie Brinkley** Girl in the Red Ferrari ◉ **John Candy** Lasky ◉ **Eddie Bracken** Roy Walley

Warner Bros., 1983 Color, 98 min.

"Getting there is half the fun!" So proclaimed Cunard Line in one of the more notable ad campaigns of the mid-twentieth century, aimed at curbing the growing popularity of air travel in favor of the traditional ocean liner. By the early 1980s, more Americans were taking vacations than ever before, but many were choosing to do so economically. Air travel was unrealistic for most families—as of 1975, only one in five Americans had ever even flown in an airplane—but cars were ubiquitous. At the beginning of *National Lampoon's Vacation*, Clark Griswold (Chevy Chase) tells his wife Ellen (Beverly D'Angelo) that he wants to drive cross-country. "The whole idea of a family vacation is to spend time together as a family," he explains. "You get on an airplane, you put on your earphones, and you're lost in your own world."

Baby Boomers like Clark were lighting out for the territory, recreating the great American road trips of their youth—back when the interstate highway system was new, and Holiday Inns and Howard Johnsons dotted the landscape. The road trip could be considered a national birthright, a twentieth-century version of Manifest Destiny. Americans, no longer able to conquer the West like their forebears, could at least traverse it. (One wonders if Clark has a brother named Lewis somewhere?)

◄ **Opposite page:** Lighting out for the territory: Rusty (Anthony Michael Hall), Clark (Chevy Chase), Ellen (Beverly D'Angelo), and Audrey Griswold (Dana Barron)

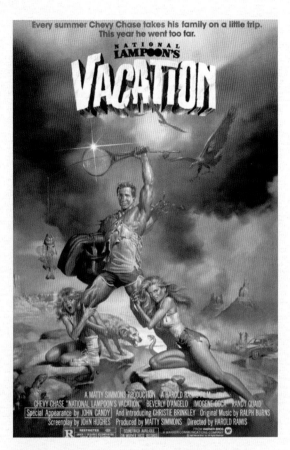

Released in July of 1983, *Vacation* topped the box office and earned an impressive $60 million.

Vacation is maybe the ultimate summer comedy. Raucously funny, it's full of absurd scenes of miscommunication and roadside mishaps. It's also a send-up of the American family, made at a time when divorce rates were at their all-time high and public figures placed a renewed emphasis on the family unit as the basis of society. With eager father Clark Griswold at the center, it is

The Griswolds arrive in Monument Valley but probably don't appreciate its beauty.

"a story of a dad," says director Harold Ramis, "who gets two weeks off a year and overcompensates like a madman to give his family everything he didn't give them for the rest of the year."

First on the agenda is to pick up the new car, but things are already not working out as Clark had planned. Told the "Antarctic blue super sports wagon" he ordered isn't yet available, he's instead offered the Wagon Queen Family Truckster, an avocado-green eyesore with wood side paneling. "You think you hate it now, but wait 'til you drive it," says the salesman (Eugene Levy) unreassuringly.

The car seems to serve them all right until Clark falls asleep at the wheel one night and veers off the highway.

They careen through a small town, narrowly missing pedestrians and other traffic before arriving, miraculously, at their motel. The car lets the midwestern family explore the country and get outside their comfort zone. A stop in Dodge City, Kansas, gives them a Wild West experience, while a detour through East St. Louis delivers a stereotyped version of the inner city (a scene that Ramis now regrets having filmed).

There's also a visit to the relatives. Ellen's cousin Catherine (Miriam Flynn) and her cheerful but dim husband, Eddie (Randy Quaid), live on a humble Kansas farm; the film pokes fun at their "state of constant recession," as Ramis puts it. To save money, they have a cookout of meatless hamburgers (but the ketchup is "nothing but the best"). Ever since Eddie was laid off from the local asbestos factory, he explains, "the bank's been after me like flies on a rib roast." Catherine is pregnant and tells Ellen that when the baby comes, "I can quit one of my night jobs." Also of note is their marijuana-growing teenage daughter, Vicki (Jane Krakowski), who is given some of the film's most outrageous dialogue. When the Griswolds escape the house the next morning, they're saddled with elderly Aunt Edna (Imogene Coca), who's headed to Phoenix with her dog, Dinky. She almost makes it there.

In an unexpected hazard of cross-country motoring, supermodel Christie Brinkley makes her film debut as a fellow highway-driver—and blonde bombshell—with whom Clark becomes obsessed. The all-American dad is probably just as aroused by her car, a bright red Ferrari 308. His iconic green station wagon—an altered Ford LTD Country Squire—was a satirical take on the large family vehicle; soon after *Vacation* was

Producer Matty Simmons says, "Everybody has a relative like Clark—a good guy who loves his family, works hard, and is anxious to do things, but he's not the brightest bulb in the lamp."

released, the minivan was introduced and caused sales of station wagons to slump, giving the film a decidedly vintage feel.

The road to California eventually delivers the Griswolds to "America's favorite family fun park," Walley World. Modeled after Disneyland—the des-

Vacation Inspiration

Load up the car and head out on the open road. Disneyland (or Six Flags Magic Mountain) makes a fitting destination, but the journey is the point. Be sure to stop at a roadside diner or two, and take in the beauty of the outdoors in one of America's iconic National Parks.

Top: Rusty and Clark enjoy some quality father-and-son time.
Middle: In-laws Eddie (Randy Quaid) and Clark
Bottom: Supermodel Christie Brinkley makes an enticing cameo.

tination in screenwriter John Hughes's original short story, "Vacation '58"—Walley World even has its own animal mascot, Marty Moose, and grandfatherly owner, Roy Walley. The park scenes were actually shot at Six Flags Magic Mountain in Valencia, California, because Disneyland wouldn't consent to its use in the film. It's easy to see why; Hughes's story begins with the line: "If Dad hadn't shot Walt Disney in the leg, it would have been our best vacation ever!" (See 1962's *40 Pounds of Trouble* for an authorized depiction.)

Hughes was a regular contributor to *National Lampoon* magazine; his story of an ill-fated family road trip was printed in the September 1979 issue. The magazine's founder, Matty Simmons, saw movie potential and brought it to Hollywood as a producer, hiring *Lampoon* veterans Chase and Ramis. Hughes would go on to write and direct a string of classic teen comedies, including *Sixteen Candles* (1984), *The Breakfast Club* (1985), and *Ferris Bueller's Day Off* (1986), becoming an auteur with a consistent theme, tone, and cast—a sort of Preston Sturges for Generation X.

Building off the popularity of *Vacation*, Hughes expanded on the lives of the Griswolds in two sequels: *National Lampoon's European Vacation* (1985) and *National Lampoon's Christmas Vacation* (1989), the latter of which has become required holiday viewing for millions.

Make It a Double Feature

Mr. Hobbs Takes a Vacation (Twentieth Century-Fox, 1962)

Twenty years before the Griswolds trekked to California, St. Louis banker Roger Hobbs (James Stewart) and his wife, Peggy (Maureen O'Hara), planned the perfect beach getaway—only to be greeted with a ramshackle cottage, a series of hijinks, and a set of unhappy family members. The film is complete with a green station wagon, a beautiful blonde (Valerie Varda) who catches Roger's eye, and Stewart's middle-American father—a spiritual predecessor to the idealistic Clark Griswold.

James Stewart and Valerie Varda

A ROOM WITH A VIEW

A young Englishwoman gets a summer education in life and love in beautiful Florence, Italy.

Director James Ivory ● **Producer** Ismail Merchant ● **Screenplay** Ruth Prawer Jhabvala, based on the book by E. M. Forster

Starring **Helena Bonham Carter** Lucy Honeychurch ● **Maggie Smith** Charlotte Bartlett
Denholm Elliott Mr. Emerson ● **Julian Sands** George Emerson
Simon Callow Mr. Beebe ● **Judi Dench** Eleanor Lavish ● **Daniel Day-Lewis** Cecil Vyse
Rosemary Leach Mrs. Honeychurch ● **Rupert Graves** Freddy Honeychurch

Curzon Film Distributors (UK), 1986 Color, 117 min.

E. M. Forster's 1908 novel *A Room with a View* is the stuff of countless high school reading lists. With appealing characters and a deceptively simple plot, it's a sort of "How I Spent My Summer Vacation" for the Edwardian set. Translated to this celebrated Merchant Ivory film, it brings to life turn-of-the-century Florence, which proves to be a most photogenic city when bathed in warm summer light.

Young Lucy Honeychurch (Helena Bonham Carter) arrives at a hotel with her chaperone, Miss Charlotte Bartlett (Maggie Smith), and is disappointed to learn she won't have a room with a view of the Arno as she expected. Their pensione is run by a British proprietor and filled with British tourists, a sign of the popularity of Florence as a cultural magnet and requisite stop along the "Grand Tour." In fact, we hardly see many Italians in the city; tourists seem to have overrun the place.

When the women venture out to explore the sights the next day, fellow traveler and author Eleanor Lavish (Judi Dench) is keen to point out the exotic Italians. "Dear simple soul," she says, referring to a wine merchant. "They're all peasants, you know." She also praises Lucy to Charlotte, noting approvingly that she seems "wide open to physical sensation." She adds that Lucy would make a fine character for her latest novel: "the young English girl transfigured by Italy."

Her prediction comes true. Lucy is jolted out of her naiveté when a shocking act of physical violence occurs in front of her in the piazza. George Emerson (Julian Sands), a young man from the pensione, rescues her from the melee and escorts her home. As the two wander back through the city, they begin to form a connection. George and his father (Denholm Elliott) represent an unbuttoned, freethinking, and unceremonious class of

The *Los Angeles Times* called *A Room with a View* "virtually irresistible."

◀ **Opposite page:** George (Julian Sands) and Lucy (Helena Bonham Carter) in the film's most romantic moment

Top: Julian Sands and Helena Bonham Carter take advantage of the pleasant summer weather.
Bottom: Julian Sands in the Loggia dei Lanzi in Florence

Briton. Charlotte is offended by their casual frankness, but Lucy is fascinated. It is the Emersons who allow Lucy a room with a view at the beginning and, through their influence, a window onto so much more. In an unashamedly romantic crescendo, George kisses her in a field of wheat.

The movie shifts to the English countryside in midsummer, when Lucy returns home to her mother (Rosemary Leach), brother Freddy (Rupert Graves), and new fiancé Cecil (Daniel Day-Lewis). It is a balmy, sun-lit world where no one seems to have a care beyond who will marry whom and where they will take tea. But Lucy is faced with a romantic quandary that will continue to play out over the course of the film.

Forster's novel, a relatively short book about youthful summer romance, has sometimes been unfairly judged light and inconsequential, at least in comparison to some of his later works, like *Howards End* (1910) and *A Passage to India* (1924). The movie plays up its immediate charms (Love! Italy!) with beautiful photography and a lush musical score. It's also quite funny, especially when broadly written characters like the anxious Charlotte and the gregarious Mr. Emerson are on screen.

A Room with a View depicts the latter days of the venerated Grand Tour, which began as an educational opportunity in the seventeenth century intended to instill qualities of independence and self-reliance while giving

A must-see city, Florence was the birthplace of the Italian Renaissance and today is one of the greatest cultural destinations in the world. It's also the capital of Tuscany, with its rolling wheat fields, vineyards, and evocative hill towns.

an immersive education in culture, statecraft, and classical antiquity. It became a rite of passage for upper-class boys to travel through France, cross the Alps, visit multiple stops in Italy—Rome, Naples, Florence, and especially Venice—and return north through Germanic Europe and the Low Countries. Women would travel as well, at first as companions to men, or for reasons of health—the need to escape dreary England for the warm climate of southern Europe. Later it became commonplace for young women to embark on the Grand Tour for their own education, often with a female chaperone.

Enter Lucy Honeychurch, who certainly gets an education and returns to England with an expanded worldview. The story contrasts stuffy social norms with the freedom to express one's emotional life. Lucy is confronted with characters who challenge her preconceptions—like the unconventional Miss Lavish, who denounces the ubiquitous Baedeker guidebook, preferring the sensual pleasures of Italy. "Smell!" she instructs Charlotte as they wander the alleyways. "A true Florentine smell. Inhale, my dear. Deeper!"

Top: Helena Bonham Carter and Daniel Day-Lewis form a respectable pair.
Bottom: "As long as I am no trouble to anyone, I have the right to do as I like," says Cecil. "It is, I dare say, an example of my decadence."

Charlotte (Maggie Smith) and Lucy (Helena Bonham Carter)

The theme of society versus the natural world is made plain in one of the film's most famous scenes, in which several of the male characters—including the vicar, Mr. Beebe (Simon Callow)—bathe in a local pond. The men frolic like children, tossing their clothes and chasing each other naked around the shallow pool, until they are embarrassingly caught by Lucy and her mother, along with the studious Cecil (all three properly bound in many layers of clothing). George Emerson is among the bathers, which accentuates the differences between him and Lucy while also adding to his free-spirited allure.

The term "Merchant Ivory" refers to the team of producer Ismail Merchant and director James Ivory and has become shorthand for a high-quality British heritage film. Their frequent screenwriting partner Ruth Prawer Jhabvala won an Oscar for *A Room with a View*, a film that epitomizes the genre: a turn-of-the-century costume drama; full of charm, wit, and class struggle; populated by the finest actors in Britain. It also made a star of Bonham Carter, who was only nineteen years old when the movie opened.

The film was shot on location in Florence and Kent in the summer of 1985, at an unusually rainy time in both places. The poor weather was, according to Simon Callow, "really disastrous for a movie that is very much dependent on the idea of the blazing sun and the blue skies." Indeed, one of the main joys of the film is seeing Italy and England in the glow of summer. The iconic opening section in Florence is the stuff of many travelers' dreams, combining incredible cultural landmarks with—thanks to Forster—the ecstasy of new love.

Make It a Double Feature

Tea with Mussolini (G2 Films, 1999)

Set a few decades after *A Room with a View*, this wartime saga of a group of eccentric British expats in Florence was shot on location by director Franco Zeffirelli and based on his own life story. Featuring another sterling cast—Maggie Smith and Judi Dench are joined by Joan Plowright, Lily Tomlin, and Cher, as a wealthy American benefactress—the movie follows the women as they raise a young Italian boy to appreciate the arts. They choose to endure the dark days of the war together in Italy, for as Dench's character says, "I have drunk deep the wine of *Firenze.*"

Judi Dench

DIRTY DANCING

A young woman spends the summer at a Catskills resort and becomes intimately involved in the lives of the staff.

Director Emile Ardolino ● **Producer** Linda Gottlieb ● **Screenplay** Eleanor Bergstein

Starring **Jennifer Grey** Frances "Baby" Houseman ● **Patrick Swayze** Johnny Castle
Cynthia Rhodes Penny Johnson ● **Jerry Orbach** Jake Houseman
Jane Brucker Lisa Houseman ● **Kelly Bishop** Marjorie Houseman
Jack Weston Max Kellerman ● **Lonny Price** Neil Kellerman ● **Max Cantor** Robbie Gould
Miranda Garrison Vivian Pressman

Vestron Pictures,
1987
Color, 100 min.

A generational touchstone, *Dirty Dancing* is a classic summer film in which "Baby" Houseman (Jennifer Grey) has a life-changing experience during a family vacation. Being more intellectual than physical, she's always played second fiddle to her beautiful sister but now opens herself up to sensations, both romantic and aerobic. The film is inspirational not just for its rousing coming-of-age story but because of its setting: the last year of the Kennedy era, when idealistic kids joined Martin Luther King Jr. in dreaming of a bright, egalitarian future. (Baby plans to join the Peace Corps.) *Dirty Dancing* takes place during "an idyllic summer," as the *New York Times* wrote, "when everything seemed possible."

In the summer of 1963, Baby arrives at Kellerman's Mountain House in the Catskills of upstate New York with her family: father Jake (Jerry Orbach), mother Marjorie (Kelly Bishop), and elder sister Lisa (Jane Brucker). Jake is friendly with the owner, Max Kellerman (Jack Weston), who sets up Baby with his grandson, Neil (Lonny Price). But she's uninterested. What does grab her attention is the resort's entertainment staff, in particular the handsome, bad-boy dance instructor Johnny Castle (Patrick Swayze), whom we soon see showing off on the dance floor with his partner, Penny (Cynthia Rhodes).

◀◀ **Opposite page:** Jennifer Grey and Patrick Swayze get closer.

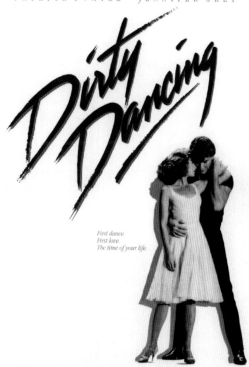

PATRICK SWAYZE · JENNIFER GREY

First dance.
First love.
The time of your life.

Dirty Dancing was the most successful release from Vestron Pictures, a short-lived studio that began in 1981 as a home video distributor.

Baby discovers that after their duties are over for the day, the staff meets at a secluded cabin to engage in "dirty dancing"—a sweaty, sexed-up atmosphere of grinding hips and gyrating torsos. There she dances with Johnny for the first time and has what could be described as a sexual awakening. When it's later revealed that Penny is pregnant and in need of an abortion, Baby agrees to take

Patrick Swayze in his most iconic role

over as Johnny's partner in an upcoming performance so that Penny can have the procedure.

Thus begins a sort of trainer-trainee relationship between Johnny and Baby, that evolves from a place of skepticism and mistrust into one of understanding, respect, and ultimately, love. Baby becomes determined to prove wrong Johnny's initial impressions and to come out of her sister's shadow, announcing her independence. "I conceived of her and made her a fighter," says screenwriter Eleanor Bergstein, "who doesn't expect the world to be handed to her." There's also a class component to their relationship: Johnny, the hired hand who's objectified as a physical specimen, versus Baby, the privileged daughter of a Jewish doctor.

Though *Dirty Dancing* was shot in North Carolina and Virginia, Kellerman's is based on the so-called "Borscht Belt" resorts of upstate New York, a nickname

for the line of Jewish-operated hotels that became popular holiday destinations for middle-class urbanites. The Catskill Mountain House had been the first to open in 1824, and many soon followed, often with explicit anti-Semitic policies. The situation was later reversed as many of the establishments came under Jewish ownership. Bergstein's own family would visit Grossinger's resort, and her memories served as inspiration for the film's plot, including late-night dirty dancing sessions with boys from outside her social circle. When asked if there was a real Johnny Castle, she replied, "I think there's one in everybody's life."

Production was put into the hands of people familiar with the world of dance. The director was documentarian Emile Ardolino, who had recently won an Oscar for *He Makes Me Feel Like Dancin'* (1983), a biographical profile of ballet dancer Jacques d'Amboise. Choreographer Kenny Ortega worked on several major projects in the 1980s, including *Xanadu* (1980), *Pretty in Pink* (1986), and the video for Madonna's "Material Girl" (1985). He would go on to direct *Newsies* (1992), *Hocus Pocus* (1993), and *High School Musical* (2006) for Disney.

Bergstein wrote the screenplay with the era's popular music in mind, and the result is a terrific compilation soundtrack that works not just to mark the era, but also to further the story and develop the characters. The music alternates between classic and contemporary styles in an anachronistic mélange of '60s nostalgia and

Top: Patrick Swayze and Jennifer Grey in the film's big finale
Middle: Johnny and Baby engage in some dirty dancing.
Bottom: Penny (Cynthia Rhodes, at right) trains her understudy.

'80s pop sensibility. It suggests that Baby is a Gen-X kid who's been dropped into an earlier time, finding inspiration from a past generation but hearing modern rhythms in her head. The movie finds its groove in the first dirty dancing sequence, thanks in large part to Berry Gordy's Motown hit "Do You Love Me," recorded by The Contours. Meanwhile, the film won an Oscar for its original song "(I've Had) The Time of My Life," performed by Bill Medley and Jennifer Warnes—a soaring duet that scores the film's rousing finale. Swayze even wrote and performed one new song himself, the power ballad "She's Like the Wind." The soundtrack album was hugely successful, going multi-platinum and spawning a second soundtrack album, *More Dirty Dancing* (1988), that also sold multiple millions.

Both of the main actors made names for themselves with this film, and they will likely always be most associated with their roles here. Jennifer Grey, the daughter of actor and dancer Joel Grey, had been in a handful of notable films at the time, including *Ferris Bueller's Day Off* (1986). She was twenty-six when she made *Dirty*

Kelly Bishop and Jerry Orbach as the Housemans

Dancing, starring opposite thirty-four-year-old Swayze, who was hired primarily because he could dance, despite his attempt to downplay his abilities because of a knee injury. The two had actually worked together once before, in the 1984 Cold War thriller *Red Dawn*.

Swayze passed away in 2009 but is still beloved by millions for his role as one of cinema's ultimate summer hunks. Although he starred in a few more memorable films—chiefly *Ghost* (1990) and *Point Break* (1991)—his signature line will always be "Nobody puts Baby in a corner."

Vacation Inspiration

There are still many resorts in the beautiful Catskills, but the main stand-in for Kellerman's was the Mountain Lake Lodge in Pembroke, Virginia. Today it offers *Dirty Dancing*–themed weekend stays, including group dance lessons and a movie location tour.

Having Wonderful Time (RKO, 1938)

Ginger Rogers leaves the city for some R&R at Camp Kare-Free, where she meets a young law school student (Douglas Fairbanks Jr.) who is working at the camp for the summer. They start off on the wrong foot, but soon have eyes for each other. Though based on a popular play, the Hays Office had the film whitewashed when adapted to the screen, with its Jewish characters renamed to appeal more to middle America. Still, it's an entertaining romp about city dwellers who escape to the great outdoors and find love waiting there.

Ginger Rogers and Douglas Fairbanks Jr.

DO THE RIGHT THING

Simmering racial tensions boil over during a hot summer day in Brooklyn.

Director Spike Lee ⚫ **Producer** Spike Lee ⚫ **Screenplay** Spike Lee

Starring **Spike Lee** Mookie ⚫ **Danny Aiello** Sal ⚫ **Giancarlo Esposito** Buggin' Out
Bill Nunn Radio Rahim ⚫ **Ossie Davis** Da Mayor ⚫ **Ruby Dee** Mother Sister
Rosie Perez Tina ⚫ **John Turturro** Pino ⚫ **Richard Edson** Vito ⚫ **Joie Lee** Jade

**Universal, 1989
Color, 120 min.**

Summer doesn't always equate to fun in the sun. It can also be a fraught season for a community—or a country—built on tribalism, when unrelenting heat and humidity test our patience. This Brooklyn-set film, full of residents we come to love and understand, illustrates some of the systemic problems facing the modern American city, from gentrification to police brutality. The prejudices of its characters have likely always existed, but the blazing heat of summer becomes the catalyst for a combative showdown between neighbors—and with the cops that aim to keep them in check. What starts as a series of racially tinged conversations becomes a charged war of words, and ultimately devolves into shocking violence.

Do the Right Thing takes place during just one particularly steamy day, on a typical block in Bedford-Stuyvesant. It opens on Samuel L. Jackson as the local deejay, Mister Señor Love Daddy, who welcomes everyone to another "HOTTT!" day in the neighborhood. Spike Lee—the film's producer, writer, and director—plays Mookie, a pizza delivery man employed by Sal (Danny Aiello), whose "famous" pizzeria has been a part of the neighborhood for a generation. One wall of his restaurant is decorated with framed photos of his favorite Italian American celebrities: Frank Sinatra, Joe DiMaggio, Al Pacino, and others. His sons, Pino (John Turturro) and Vito (Richard Edson), are foils for Mookie;

they work alongside him out of respect for their father, but Pino especially is openly hostile toward Mookie and the other black residents.

Across the street is a Korean-owned grocery store, whose proprietors (played by Steve Park and Ginny Yang) don't yet have a full grasp of English. Young Puerto Ricans hang out at the other end of the block, while a small Greek chorus of men (Paul Benjamin, Frankie Faison, and Robin Harris) sit in lawn chairs on the sidewalk, commenting on the comings and goings.

◀ **Opposite page:** Buggin' Out (Giancarlo Esposito) and others confront Clifton (John Savage), one of the neighborhood's few white residents.

Rosie Perez in her film debut as Mookie's exasperated girlfriend, Tina

seen it all. The two stars, married in real life, represent the heritage of black filmmaking and a symbolic passing of the torch to Spike Lee.

There are also two wandering philosopher figures. Radio Raheem (Bill Nunn), who carries around a boom box that serves as an extension of his personality, explains his brass knuckles that read "LOVE" and "HATE" in an urban homage to *The Night of the Hunter* (1955). A disabled man, Smiley (Roger Guenveur Smith), sells photographs of Martin Luther King Jr. and Malcolm X to his neighbors—a reminder of the civil rights era and the dreams of a generation.

The interaction of these personalities is what drives the movie forward, but the central conflict is kicked off when Buggin' Out (Giancarlo Esposito) confronts Sal one day about his photographs. "How come there ain't no brothers up on the wall?" he asks. "Rarely do I see any Italian Americans eating in here. All I see is black folks." He pushes for a boycott of the pizzeria, while most of the residents roll their eyes at him. But the tensions of this moment snowball, leading to an explosive final act and some thorny moral implications. At one point, Da Mayor stops Mookie on the street to impart a bit of wisdom. "Always do the right thing," he says. "That's it?" Mookie asks. "I got it. I'm gone."

This isn't the New York of films like *Wall Street* (1987) and *Working Girl* (1988), with its booming stock portfolios. Every day is a grind in Bed-Stuy. Since

The white cops roll by every now and then, casting suspicious glances at everyone.

Two elderly residents serve as a connection to the city's past. Da Mayor (Ossie Davis), a functioning alcoholic, asks Sal for one-off jobs to scrape together a little spending money; Mother Sister (Ruby Dee) sits jadedly at the window of her brownstone like a woman who's air-conditioning is an unknown luxury, the kids go to the street to play in an open fire hydrant—drawing consternation from the cops, who put an end to the fun. Mookie takes a midday break to have a cold shower, and his girlfriend, Tina (Rosie Perez), dips her face into a bowl of ice water. Even the film's musical score (by Bill Lee, Spike's father) seems to be affected by the heat, with a saxophone that slides unenergetically up and down the scale. The cinematography (by Ernest Dickerson) emphasizes warm reds and golds, giving the neighborhood an oven-like glow.

Summer has historically been a season for racial unrest and activism across the United States, from the 1921 Tulsa race massacre, to Mississippi's Freedom Summer, to the 1965 Watts riots, to the 2020 protests against the murder of George Floyd by Minneapolis police. When *Do the Right Thing* was released in July 1989, a few commentators worried openly that its incendiary subject matter and tone would lead to race riots. The film is "playing with dynamite in an urban playground," wrote one film critic. "If some audiences go wild, [Lee is] partly responsible." Filmmaker Paul Schrader responded, in a *New York Times* roundtable on the film: "Art doesn't need to be responsible. Art can be incendiary. Art can be inflammatory. Spike has been held to an extraordinary level of responsibility, and he has risen to it. Which was more than we should ever ask of any artist, and to his great credit that he did."

Top: Mother Sister (Ruby Dee) and Da Mayor (Ossie Davis)
Bottom: Pino (John Turturro) antagonizes Mookie (Spike Lee).

Spike Lee was part of a wave of independent black filmmakers that included Robert Townsend, Euzhan Palcy, and Charles Lane. His first film, *She's Gotta Have It* (1986), was shot in just twelve days with a budget of $175,000. He would come to be known for his authentic films about race in America, including *Malcolm X* (1992), the documentary *4 Little Girls* (1997), and *BlacKkKlansman* (2018), which won Lee an Oscar for its screenplay.

Vacation Inspiration

As the movie predicted, Brooklyn is being gentrified. But it's still a diverse melting pot of cultures, well worth exploring. The block of Bed-Stuy where the film was made has been renamed "Do The Right Thing Way"—it's on Stuyvesant Ave. between Quincy St. and Lexington Ave.

Hopefully this movie will one day become a relic of the nation's troubled past, showing us how far we have come. But in the decades since its release, Lee's film has remained sadly relevant, revealing a world of anxieties, fears, and hopes that will likely feel familiar to many viewers today. It was dedicated in 1989 to the families of several black victims of police violence; to this list we can add Michael Brown, Philando Castile, Breonna Taylor, Eric Garner, Tamir Rice, George Floyd, and countless others. *Do the Right Thing* continues to be one of the most stimulating and thought-provoking racial dramas ever made in America, packaged as an entertainment but offering no easy answers.

Top: Mookie (Spike Lee) and Sal (Danny Aiello), with the Italian American "Wall of Fame" in the background
Bottom: Da Mayor tells Mookie, "Always do the right thing."

Radio Raheem (Bill Nunn) carries his namesake boom box.

Crooklyn (Universal, 1994)

Set in the summer of 1973 in Bedford-Stuyvesant, this Spike Lee "joint" is based on the director's own childhood experiences. Alfre Woodard and Delroy Lindo play the loving (and often bickering) parents, but the main characters are the kids, including young sister Troy (Zelda Harris), who could roam the neighborhood—playing hopscotch and skipping rope—in the years before drugs and crime made the streets unsafe for play. One of this nostalgic film's highlights is its period soundtrack, a greatest hits of '70s soul and R&B.

Delroy Lindo, Alfre Woodard, and family

A LEAGUE OF THEIR OWN

During World War II, a pair of sisters become professional baseball players and go all the way to the championship.

Director Penny Marshall   **Producers** Elliot Abbott and Robert Greenhut

Screenplay Lowell Ganz and Babaloo Mandel, based on a story by Kim Wilson and Kelly Candaele

Starring **Geena Davis** Dottie Hinson   **Lori Petty** Kit Keller

Tom Hanks Jimmy Dugan   **Madonna** Mae Mordabito   **Rosie O'Donnell** Doris Murphy

Megan Cavanagh Marla Hooch   **David Strathairn** Ira Lowenstein

Garry Marshall Walter Harvey   **Jon Lovitz** Ernie Capadino

Columbia, 1992
Color, 128 min.

Baseball is the iconic summertime sport. A game with no timer, just nine leisurely innings—or more, if needed; it's perfect for long summer days and balmy evenings. Among the many movies about America's pastime over the past century, few are as entertaining and inspirational as *A League of Their Own*. It also happens to be an outlier: it's about the many talented women who stepped into the spotlight while the male players from major and minor leagues were away at war.

The All-American Girls Professional Baseball League's first season consisted of 108 games played between late May and early September of 1943, followed by a playoff series. It quickly expanded and continued for over a decade, during which time this film's central team, the Rockford Peaches, won a league-best four championships. The movie draws loosely on this history to create a rousing story about the intrepid women athletes who—in the case of the main characters—left their small town for the big city and found fame as professional ballplayers.

The story opens in Oregon's Willamette Valley in 1943, where sisters Dottie Hinson (Geena Davis) and Kit Keller (Lori Petty) work on their family farm. They also play softball for a local team—Kit as a pitcher, Dottie as catcher—and are discovered by Ernie Capadino (Jon

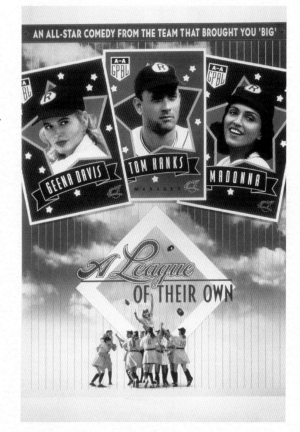

Penny Marshall's earlier film *Big* (1988) was the first release by a woman director to earn $100 million at the box office.

Lovitz), who is scouting talent for the professional women's league. He wants to recruit Dottie, who isn't interested in leaving home while her husband is away at war. But Kit wants an escape from their small town. "Don't you want to say you once did something?" Kit asks her sister. "I've got to get out of here. I'm nothing here." In solidarity, Dottie agrees to go.

◀◀ **Previous page:** Dottie (Geena Davis) at bat

The film introduces the "candy bar king" Walter Harvey (Garry Marshall), a thinly veiled substitute for chewing gum mogul and Chicago Cubs owner Philip K. Wrigley. Dottie and Kit make it to "Harvey Field" (shot at Wrigley Field) for the tryouts, a gathering of dozens of great players whose talent makes the notion of a women's league immediately seem viable. They end up together on the Rockford Peaches along with friendly first baseman Helen (Anne Ramsay), shortstop

Jimmy (Tom Hanks) and Doris (Rosie O'Donnell)

and beauty contest winner Ellen Sue (Freddie Simpson), and right fielder Evelyn (Bitty Schram), who brings her annoying son Stilwell (Justin Scheller) on the road with her. There's also a pair of earthy friends from New York, brash Doris (Rosie O'Donnell) and worldly Mae (Madonna), who is nicknamed "All the Way" Mae. The movie plays up Madonna's real-life bad-girl reputation; at one point she helps an illiterate teammate learn to read using an erotic book.

Another memorable player is Marla Hooch (Megan Cavanagh), a terrific ambidextrous batter who makes the team despite not living up to the standards of beauty the league seeks. Even her father admits that she "ain't as pretty as these other girls." Her inelegant appearance is played for laughs, like when a charm school instructor recommends "a lot of night games." Her character could be Exhibit A in the film's larger theme of society's expectations of women. In one scene, a female radio commentator decries the "masculinization of women" in Harvey's league. "When our boys come home from war, what kind of girls will they be coming home to?"

One night the team manages to sneak off to a roadhouse for some mixed company. While Mae—a dancehall girl back in New York—shows off her skills, it's Marla who wins the night. She takes the stage and drunkenly croons "It Had to Be You" to a lovestruck man. When Dottie asks what happened, Doris says, "We just gave her a dress." Mae giggles, "And a lot of liquor."

recalled how she and her teammates "were expected to look like Betty Grable and play ball like DiMaggio." *A League of Their Own* attempts to lay bare the absurd double standards facing female athletes. Who cares if they're "ladylike" if they can play killer ball?

The movie is also a story of sisterhood and the tensions that develop between Dottie and Kit, the latter of whom seems doomed to live in the shadow of her talented, beautiful, married older sister. Even back home in Oregon, their game ends with Dottie "bailing out" Kit with a home run. When they get to the professional league, Dottie gets nicknamed "The Queen of Diamonds" and makes the cover of *Life* magazine, but Kit never can seem to get the respect she deserves.

The dual themes of the film work seamlessly together, thanks to skillful direction of Penny Marshall, one of the few women directors working on major Hollywood productions at the time. Though she became famous in the '70s for her role on *Laverne & Shirley*, she had recently begun to direct feature films, including the box-office hit *Big* (1988) and Best Picture nominee *Awakenings* (1990). With *A League of Their Own*, Marshall found the biggest hit of her career.

Top: Tom Hanks and Geena Davis
Bottom: Jimmy tells Evelyn (Bitty Schram), "There's no crying in baseball!"

The league itself advertises the beauty of its players to sell tickets, giving them skimpy uniforms—what Mae calls "half a dress"—and having them participate in promotional stunts that show off both their legs and their homemaking skills. Real-life player Lois Youngen later

The central male role in the film is that of team manager Jimmy Dugan, played memorably by Tom Hanks. The character of an alcoholic former slugger was based on Jimmie Foxx, a three-time American League MVP and one of the all-time home run hitters. Jimmy's story

arc sees him regain legitimacy while finding respect for the women he manages. His incredulous line "There's no crying in baseball!" has become a classic in both the film and sports worlds.

When the film came out in 1992, *Chicago Sun-Times* critic Roger Ebert began his review with an admission that until seeing the movie, "I had no idea that an organization named the All-American Girls Professional Baseball League ever flourished in this country." When it was disbanded in 1954, "it was consigned to oblivion; history is written by the victors." Thanks in large part to Marshall, the League has come out of the shadows, and it has been inspiring generations of athletes ever since.

Left: Sisters Kit (Lori Petty) and Dottie (Geena Davis)
Above: "All the Way" Mae (Madonna)

Vacation Inspiration

Visit Cooperstown, New York, home of the National Baseball Hall of Fame and Museum, whose 1988 exhibit "Women in Baseball" helped to inspire Marshall's film. Or just play a leisurely game of catch in the backyard—you'll want to after watching this movie.

Bend It Like Beckham (Helkon SK, 2002)

This British culture-clash film tells of teenage soccer player Jess Bhamra (Parminder Nagra), whose conservative Indian family is critical of her pastime. Jess, whose idol is star footballer David Beckham, is a skilled player and is recruited by another young athlete, Jules (Keira Knightley), to play on a girls' team for the summer. The Hounslow Harriers soon become one of the best teams in the league and even travel to a competition in Germany, but all the while Jess lies to her parents about her involvement in the sport. This inspiring film comes from director Gurinder Chadha, who drew on her own experiences growing up Asian in West London: "What I did my whole life was bend the rules."

Keira Knightley and Parminder Nagra

BEFORE SUNRISE

Two young strangers meet on a train to Vienna and spend a romantic night wandering the city.

Director Richard Linklater ● **Producer** Anne Walker-McBay
Screenplay Kim Krizan and Richard Linklater

Starring **Ethan Hawke** Jesse ● **Julie Delpy** Céline ● **Erni Mangold** Palm Reader
Dominik Castell Street Poet ● **Haymon Maria Buttinger** Bartender

Columbia, 1995
Color, 101 min.

Backpacking through Europe is a time-honored summer tradition for many middle-class young people eager to see the world on a budget. Twenty-five-year-old Jesse (Ethan Hawke) is on one such journey of discovery but also seemingly adrift in a post-college funk. When Céline (Julie Delpy) first sees him on a train from Budapest to Vienna, she gets a clue to his real problem: he's reading a book titled *All I Need Is Love.*

The *New York Times* described this film as a "Eurail Pass version of *An Affair to Remember,*" and there's something to that analogy. Both films are about finding love in transit—the in-between spaces of life—and feature romantically unsatisfied characters who connect with strangers they meet along their journey.

Before Sunrise is perhaps the most down-to-earth love story ever put to film. The stakes are low, as is the melodrama. Hawke calls it "a romance for realists," because Jesse and Céline—both charmingly broke and street-smart—make a spontaneous but not irresponsible decision to be together. It begins with a meet-cute in which they find themselves sitting across from each other on the train after a bickering couple leads Céline to abandon her original seat. She asks if he's on holiday. "I don't really know what I'm on," he says. After a long chat, Jesse proposes an "admittedly insane idea," that they get off the train together and spend his last night in

Before Sunrise was followed by *Before Sunset* (2004) and *Before Midnight* (2013).

Europe exploring Vienna. He has a flight home the next morning; she's on her way back to school in Paris and can, he suggests, go tomorrow just as easily as today. He charms her and she impulsively agrees. She doesn't even know his name yet. Their first few minutes together are both a rush—*Let's do this!*—and awkward—*Have we made a big mistake?*—until they begin to talk.

And talk they do. Their discussions are richer and more revealing than what most movie characters are usually given. They wander and talk about their

Jesse (Ethan Hawke)

insecurities, their philosophies, their earliest memories, the realities of love, generational struggles, and even the war in Bosnia. And through this long conversation they build a relationship based on personality and intellect as much as physical attraction.

Yet there are still some moments of whimsy, like when Céline hires a fortune-teller at an outdoor café. "You are an adventurer, a seeker," the palmist (Erni Mangold) tells her in broken English. "You need to resign yourself to the awkwardness of life. Only if you find peace within yourself will you find true connection with others." And at sunset, Jesse and Céline share their first kiss at the top of a Ferris wheel—a nod to *The Third Man* (1949).

The film's key scene takes place at a floating restaurant, where Céline admits, "After tomorrow morning, we're probably never going to see each other again, right?" Jesse is startled, but recognizes it's likely true.

"Let's just be rational adults about this," she says. "It's not so bad if tonight is our only night, right?" He agrees. "No delusions, no projections. We'll just make tonight great." It's a profoundly bittersweet decision that somehow feels both mature and naive.

The movie is full of possibilities, both immediate—where to wander, what to eat—and long-term—*Where are we going with our lives? Will we ever meet again?* The film's title, evoking dawn, suggests that a new day lies ahead for the characters, a world fresh with opportunity. Not an end, but a beginning.

Before Sunrise became the first entry in a series of films about Jesse and Céline. After a gap of nine years, they reunite in *Before Sunset* (2004) and wander the streets of Paris while talking about how—in their thirties—they now view the world with adult eyes. *Before Midnight* (2013) takes place in Greece and shows them firmly in middle age: a little older, a little wiser,

Céline (Julie Delpy)

Ethan Hawke and Julie Delpy explore the Imperial City.

a little more cynical. These highly acclaimed sequels invite a reevaluation of the first film. Seen by itself, it's a sweet whirlwind romance. But when viewed in the context of one's whole life, youth's unencumbered pleasures gain extra poignancy.

The film was based on an experience director Richard Linklater had with a woman several years earlier in Philadelphia, in which they similarly spent the night walking around the city together. He immediately saw the potential for a movie capturing the spontaneity of the moment and the serendipitous connection he found with another person. "I think I have a low threshold of what a movie can be," says Linklater, regarding the film's long conversational scenes. "I'm kind of a minimalist." He eventually wrote the screenplay with a female friend, Kim Krizan, in order to balance the gender perspective. A lot of the dialogue was rewritten by the actors as they rehearsed and shot over twenty-five days in Vienna in the summer of 1994. Linklater has since made other movies that creatively engage with time. Most notably, his 2014 film *Boyhood*, filmed bit by bit over a twelve-year period, shows a young man age into adulthood across the course of the film.

Before Sunrise was part of a fertile wave of independent filmmaking in America in the 1990s, yet Linklater's movie also had the backing of a major distributor (Columbia) even before it premiered at the Sundance Film Festival in 1995. An example of what has been termed "Indiewood" cinema, it was made at once with the support of the studio system and—by virtue of its limitations in form and style—in opposition to it.

As a summer film, however, it is quite typical. It suggests how travel, like Jesse's ramble through Europe, can open us up to new faces and new perspectives. Summer is a season of self-discovery that reveals what is missing from our everyday lives. If we were all blessed with the ability to connect with others as easily as Jesse and Céline do, imagine how different life might be.

Top: Céline and Jesse hop off the train in Vienna . . .
Bottom: . . . and jump in a streetcar.

Vacation Inspiration

Vienna is a beautiful city and a cultural capital, full of imperial history, classical music, and stunning architecture. A great way to explore it would be by taking a *Before Sunrise*–themed walking tour of its many filming locations.

The Green Ray (Les Films du Losange, 1986)

Eric Rohmer's films are largely driven by the conversations of their characters, and that's true of this summertime story about a newly single woman, Delphine (Marie Rivière), who is forced to vacation alone when her traveling companion backs out at the last minute. Self-conscious and introverted, she is unable to enjoy herself on the beaches of Biarritz. But like Jesse in *Before Sunrise*, she forms an unexpected connection with a stranger (Vincent Gauthier) just as she is about to leave. The film's title refers to a rare atmospheric phenomenon—and a good omen for Delphine—in which the setting sun gives off a flash of green light just as it disappears over the horizon.

Vincent Gauthier and Marie Rivière

MOONRISE KINGDOM

A young scout and his female pen pal run away together and camp on a deserted beach.

Director Wes Anderson ● **Producers** Wes Anderson, Jeremy Dawson, Steven Rales, and Scott Rudin ● **Screenplay** Wes Anderson and Roman Coppola

Starring **Jared Gilman** Sam Shakusky ● **Kara Hayward** Suzy Bishop
Edward Norton Scout Master Ward ● **Bruce Willis** Captain Sharp
Bill Murray Walt Bishop ● **Frances McDormand** Laura Bishop ● **Bob Balaban** The Narrator
Jason Schwartzman Cousin Ben ● **Lucas Hedges** Redford ● **Tilda Swinton** Social Services

Focus Features,
2012
Color, 94 min.

Wes Anderson has become a celebrated auteur for his postmodern creations, unconventional stories told with wit and eccentricity. In *Moonrise Kingdom*, he trains his camera on a pair of young misfits who traverse the fictional island of New Penzance in the summer of 1965. As described by a tongue-in-cheek promotional ad for the film, it's "a touching story of two misunderstood young lovers on the run. It's got thrills, adventure, comedy, romance, Bruce Willis, and you might find yourself moved to tears."

The film begins in a most Andersonian fashion, as the camera glides through the home of Suzy Bishop (Kara Hayward), drifting down hallways and floating between floors to reveal a series of quaintly appointed rooms and the various family members. It's a rainy day, and Suzy uses her binoculars to survey the outside world. Through an on-screen narrator (Bob Balaban) we're introduced to the island, its environment, its inhabitants—and the film's ironic tone: hyper-stylized but sincere. The Bishop family live in a house called "Summer's End," and the film takes place in the first few days of September.

Raising Suzy has been a chore for her parents, Laura (Frances McDormand) and Walt (Bill Murray), as Suzy discovers one day when she comes across a book called *Coping with the Very Troubled Child*. "I am in trouble

◀◀ **Previous page:** Suzy (Kara Hayward) and Sam (Jared Gilman)

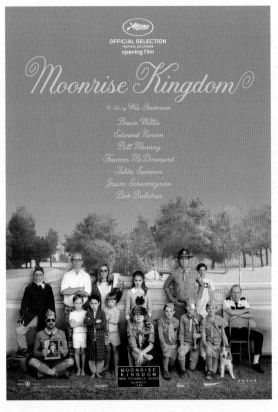

Moonrise Kingdom opened the 2012 Cannes Film Festival and was later nominated for the Oscar for Best Original Screenplay.

again because I threw a rock through the window," she writes in a letter to a friend. "My mother still has glass in her hair." Unbeknownst to the parents, her pen pal is a boy she met the previous year, Sam Shakusky (Jared Gilman), and she is planning to run away with him. Sam has some behavioral issues, too. "I accidentally built a fire while I was sleepwalking," he writes. "I have no memory of this, but my foster parents think I am lying."

He lives in a boys' home and is considered to be "emotionally disturbed."

Sam is a member of the Khaki Scouts and is spending the summer at Camp Ivanhoe with his troop, though he doesn't really get along with any of them. When Scout Master Randy Ward (Edward Norton) discovers that Sam has run away during the night, he deputizes an older camper (Lucas Hedges) and sends out a search party. "I heard he ran away because his family died," says one Scout. "I heard he never had any family in the first place," says another. "That's probably why he's crazy."

Sam and Suzy are able to evade them, though. They set up camp in a secluded bay, swim in the sea, listen to records (Suzy packed a turntable). He does watercolors.

She explains her fascination with binoculars. "It helps me see things closer, even if they're not very far away. I pretend it's my magic power." They also discover what it feels like to fall in love, and they dance together on the rocky shore. But their little utopia isn't to be. The island's police officer, Captain Sharp (Willis), and a social services worker (Tilda Swinton) are both after Sam, and the whole affair is soon complicated by a massive storm that rolls in during the film's second half.

Anderson's films are often called "quirky" due to his idiosyncratic characters, retro music, and tableau-like visual style. He designs conspicuously artificial worlds and populates them with lovable nonconformists. His

Sam with Captain Sharp (Bruce Willis)

Rhode Island's Narragansett Bay provided the outdoor locations for *Moonrise Kingdom*, including the beach at Fort Wetherill State Park on Conanicut Island. While exploring the area, check out the Conanicut Island Light—used for the exterior of Suzy's house—and Newport's Trinity Church, which is featured in the film's second half.

movies are filled with interesting objects, often with a vintage twist. *Moonrise Kingdom* features not just period clothing and housewares, but also unique items like Suzy's collection of stolen library books, with original cover art developed for the film. The camera often exaggerates things further by its playful tilts, zoom shots, and generally detached gaze.

Anderson applies a plaintive tone to many of his films, usually in contrast to the visual style; consider the highly successful but depressive family in *The Royal Tenenbaums* (2001). At one point in *Moonrise Kingdom*, Bill Murray's character wanders shirtless through the

Scout Master Ward (Edward Norton) with two Khaki Scouts (Gabriel Rush and Joshua Meehan)

background with an open bottle of wine. He retrieves an ax from a broom closet and announces to his young sons that he's going to find a tree to chop down. It's a moment of discontent, played dryly for laughs. Anderson treats all his characters—even the youngest kids—with respect and honesty, and their stories are told with an air of sweet optimism. His work is often surreal but rarely cynical.

The music of Benjamin Britten is used throughout the film, beginning with an opening scene scored to *The Young Person's Guide to the Orchestra*. The 1945 composition was designed to be an introduction to the various instrumental sections—woodwinds, brass, percussion—illustrating how the individual parts of an orchestra serve the whole, which is Wes Anderson's eclectic style in a nutshell. This bit of midcentury British orderliness works well with the American film director's obsessively managed screen compositions. Later on, Britten's short opera about Noah's Ark, *Noye's Fludde*, is performed in flashback—revealing how Sam and Suzy met and foreshadowing the devastating storm.

Top: Suzy (Kara Hayward)
Bottom: Mr. Bishop (Bill Murray)

Moonrise Kingdom was shot on 16mm film using handheld cameras, evoking the feel and spirit of the French New Wave, a movement that's contemporaneous to this film's setting. For a filmmaker like François Truffaut, whose *The 400 Blows* (1959) foregrounds rebellious youth, these new cameras represented a freedom of production, and by extension, new possibilities of the cinema. *Moonrise Kingdom* shares that sense of adventure and opportunity, all within a whimsical movie set fifty years in the past.

Left: Bob Balaban serves as the film's on-screen narrator.

Make It a Double Feature

Bill Murray and Harvey Atkin (right)

Meatballs (Paramount, 1979)

Thirty years earlier, Bill Murray starred as counselor Tripper Harrison in this hit movie about a second-rate summer camp and its colorful staff. Tripper takes a shy new camper, Rudy (Chris Makepeace), under his wing and they strike up a friendship. When the camp later faces off against its wealthy neighbor, Camp Mohawk, in the annual "Olympiad," a newly confident Rudy saves the day. Ivan Reitman had his directorial breakout with *Meatballs*, from a screenplay cowritten by *Caddyshack* (1980) director Harold Ramis—both of whom would later work together with Murray on *Stripes* (1981) and *Ghostbusters* (1985).

CALL ME BY YOUR NAME

A young man in Italy falls in love with a visiting graduate student during the summer of 1983.

Director Luca Guadagnino ● **Producers** Emilie Georges, Luca Guadagnino, James Ivory, Marco Morabito, Howard Rosenman, Peter Spears, and Rodrigo Teixeira
Screenplay James Ivory, from the novel by André Aciman

Starring **Timothée Chalamet** Elio Perlman ● **Armie Hammer** Oliver

Michael Stuhlbarg Mr. Perlman ● **Amira Casar** Mrs. Perlman ● **Esther Garrel** Marzia

Victoire Du Bois Chiara ● **Vanda Capriolo** Mafalda ● **Antonio Rimoldi** Anchise

Sony Pictures Classics, 2017
Color, 132 min.

Seventeen-year-old Elio Perlman (Timothée Chalamet), lithe and tousle-headed, lives a charmed life. He spends the long summer days playing music, lying out in the sun, and reading books by a quiet pond. The only son of an archaeology professor (Michael Stuhlbarg) who works from a villa in northern Italy, Elio inhabits a comfortable, carefree world in which people are able to focus on matters of the heart. One rainy afternoon his mother (Amira Casar) reads him a story about a lovelorn knight who is too timid to declare his love for a beautiful princess. "Is it better to speak or to die?" asks the young knight. The story is prescient, for Elio has met another young man and will soon be faced with the knight's dilemma: will he confess his desire or suffer in anguish?

Call Me by Your Name, an almost meditative portrait of a languid summer from Italian director Luca Guadagnino, isn't heavy on plot. Its strengths lie in its indelible moments: a standoff at a war monument, a wise speech from father to son, a cathartic gaze into a fireplace. It's about the simple pleasures of an outdoor breakfast on a sunny morning and a baroque piano serenade. The atmosphere is seductive, and the story's promise of romance serves to imbue with meaning every stray glance, every touch, and every word spoken.

◄ **Previous page:** Armie Hammer and Timothée Chalamet in Crema's Piazza del Duomo

The Perlmans' villa is a character unto itself. It's an ancient place, with timeworn frescoes and an eclectic mix of antique furniture that feels deliberately bohemian. The windows seem to be permanently open, and the family—"neither stuffy nor rich people," per the director—live as much outdoors as in. Elio is seen gazing pensively across windowsills and leaning over wrought-iron balconies. Each summer, they invite a

Screenwriter James Ivory won the Oscar for Best Adapted Screenplay.

graduate student to assist with research, and at the beginning of the film they welcome Oliver (Armie Hammer) into their cultured but unpretentious world.

Though Elio carries on with a local girl, Marzia (Esther Garrel)—they dance together at the disco, swim in the lake at night, and sneak off for some alone time whenever they get the chance—he becomes intrigued by the handsome male visitor. It's not clear that Elio knows how to label his feelings, but Oliver—at first just an agreeable companion—begins to occupy more and more of his thoughts. "I was too harsh," he scribbles in a journal. "I thought he didn't like me."

Elio is a musician and often sits at a table with headphones on, pencil in hand, transcribing classical pieces into piano notation. One day in the garden he plays a simple Bach melody on the guitar and Oliver compliments him. Elio beckons him to the piano inside, where he teases him by playing increasingly embellished versions of the piece. "Play *that* again," insists Oliver, "the thing you played outside." He leaves in a huff, but when Elio finally plays the original, he returns and listens, captivated.

Mr. Perlman takes them out to Lake Garda, where a sunken bronze is being raised to the surface. The sculpture is a copy of an original by Praxiteles, the "greatest sculptor in antiquity," Mr. Perlman notes approvingly. The boys run their hands over it, fascinated by its history and beauty. Later, while cataloging slides of classical

Top: Timothée Chalamet and Esther Garrel
Middle: Elio in a moment of ennui
Bottom: Michael Stuhlbarg as the wise and cheerful Mr. Perlman

statuary, Mr. Perlman gives a description of their sensuality that could apply just as easily to Oliver. "Not a straight body in these statues. They're all curved," he says. "And so nonchalant. Hence their ageless ambiguity.

Elio (Timothée Chalamet) exaggerates a Bach piece, to the frustration of Oliver (Armie Hammer).

As if they're daring you to desire them." Oliver sits quietly by, appearing flushed.

The movie is hedonistic, full of leisurely outdoor meals, bike rides down country roads, swimming in secluded lakes, famished kisses. There's also an infamous scene involving a peach, that's at once a bit kinky and expressive of Elio's abiding innocence. Through these scenes, the film connects Elio's desires and passions to the natural world.

Based on André Aciman's 2007 novel, which was set on the Italian Riviera, the film was moved northeast to Lombardy. Filming took place in and around the town of Crema, where Elio and Oliver bike through quiet, sunbaked streets and relax in the piazza. Screenwriter and veteran filmmaker James Ivory had experience adapting literary texts, including Italian-set *A Room with a View* (1986). His screenplay incorporates bouts of silence that are as important as the dialogue. Elio's taciturn glares and quiet prowls around the house—messing with Oliver's swim trunks, for instance—are some of the ways the film most effectively reveals its characters.

It also makes clever use of the soundtrack, with a mixture of classical music, reflecting Elio's hobby; '80s pop, reflecting the larger society around him; and new songs by Sufjan Stevens, reflecting his inner life. One of these new songs plays over an incredibly moving final shot that lasts throughout the entire end credits sequence.

Though the setting seems to exist outside of time, the film is explicitly set in the summer of 1983—made apparent through its clothing, cars, and Walkmans. Temporality becomes a narrative force, as in a sequence where Elio spends a day checking his watch before meeting Oliver at midnight. Film critic Molly Haskell writes that the film "skillfully captures both the languor of the summer mood, as time stretches into boredom,

Vacation Inspiration

Lombardy is one of the premier Italian regions for travelers, anchored by the cultural and financial capital of Milan. East of the city are Crema, Bergamo, Lake Garda, and more of the film's evocative locations.

Timothée Chalamet and Armie Hammer at Lake Garda

and the simultaneous feel of time closing in, of the possibility of missed opportunities." Oliver's summer with the Perlmans has an expiration date, and one of the film's lessons is how we should take advantage of the opportunities given to us.

Summer vacation—like a microcosm of life—is limited, with time ever running out. Time for anything. Time for romance. Time for self-discovery. Time to tell others who you are. Mr. Perlman counsels Elio to not block out the emotions and desires he feels, however miserable they make him. "Our hearts and our bodies are given to us only once," he says, ruefully. "And before you know it, your heart's worn out."

"So, does he speak?" Oliver asks of the lovelorn knight. "No," says Elio. "He fudges." But soon afterward—at the town's war memorial, a poignant reminder of the fragility of life—Elio finds his courage and speaks.

A thoughtful Oliver (Armie Hammer), with Elio (Timothée Chalamet) in the background

Pride (Twentieth Century-Fox, 2014)

This heartwarming British film, set over the course of a year in the 1980s, begins and ends with the London Pride Parade and—unlike *Call Me by Your Name*—features characters who openly identify as members of the LGBTQ community. The main storyline follows the formation of "Lesbians and Gays Support the Miners," a real-life solidarity group that raised money for families affected by a 1984 strike. But it's also an engaging set of personal stories, including the coming-out of a young student (George MacKay) who joins the group and, like Elio, finds his voice. It's the perfect movie for Pride Month, a celebration of hard-won social victories and an ever-expanding community of allies.

Faye Marsay, George MacKay, Ben Schnetzer (above), Joe Gilgun, and Paddy Considine

BIBLIOGRAPHY

This list comprises books cited and consulted, plus a listing of periodicals, scholarly journals, and various online resources. In addition, information was gathered from the many documentaries and supplemental features included on home video releases for the films in this book.

BOOKS

Altman, Rick. *The American Film Musical*. Bloomington: Indiana University Press, 1987.

Armes, Roy. *French Cinema*. New York: Oxford University Press, 1985.

Babington, Bruce. *The Sports Film: Games People Play*. New York: Wallflower, 2014.

Barrios, Richard. *Must-See Musicals: 50 Show-Stopping Movies We Can't Forget*. Philadelphia: Running Press, 2017.

Basinger, Jeanine. *The Movie Musical!* New York: Knopf, 2019.

———. *The Star Machine*. New York: Knopf, 2007.

Bellos, David. *Jacques Tati: His Life and Art*. London: Harvill, 1999.

Bergman, Ingmar. *Images: My Life in Film*. Translated by Marianne Ruuth. New York: Arcade, 1994.

Bogle, Donald. *Hollywood Black: The Stars, the Films, the Filmmakers*. Philadelphia: Running Press, 2019.

Brill, Leslie. *John Huston's Filmmaking*. Cambridge, UK: Cambridge University Press, 1997.

Browning, Mark. *Wes Anderson: Why His Movies Matter*. Santa Barbara, CA: Praeger, 2011.

Brownlow, Kevin. *David Lean: A Biography*. New York: St. Martin's, 1996.

Carr, Jay, ed. *The A List: The National Society of Film Critics' 100 Essential Films*. New York: Da Capo, 2002.

Clarke, Gerald. *Get Happy: The Life of Judy Garland*. New York: Delta, 2000.

Coleman, Marilyn, and Lawrence H. Ganong, eds. *The Social History of the American Family: An Encyclopedia*. Thousand Oaks, CA: Sage, 2014.

Considine, David. *The Cinema of Adolescence*. Jefferson, NC: McFarland, 1985.

Davis, Blair. *The Battle for the Bs: 1950s Hollywood and the Rebirth of Low-Budget Cinema*. New Brunswick, NJ: Rutgers University Press, 2012.

De Semlyen, Nick. *Wild and Crazy Guys: How the Comedy Mavericks of the '80s Changed Hollywood Forever*. New York: Crown Archetype, 2019.

Delaney, Tim, and Tim Madigan. *Lessons Learned from Popular Culture*. Albany: SUNY Press, 2016.

Dick, Bernard F. *The Merchant Prince of Poverty Row: Harry Cohn of Columbia Pictures*. Lexington: University Press of Kentucky, 1993.

Dilley, Whitney Crothers. *The Cinema of Wes Anderson: Bringing Nostalgia to Life*. New York: Wallflower, 2017.

Dixon, Wheeler W., and Gwendolyn Audrey Foster. *A Short History of Film*, 3rd ed. New Brunswick, NJ: Rutgers University Press, 2018.

Doherty, Thomas. *Teenagers and Teenpics: The Juvenilization of American Movies in the 1950s*. Philadelphia: Temple University Press, 2002.

Dutton, Julian. *Keeping Quiet: Visual Comedy in the Age of Sound*. Gosport, UK: Chaplin Books, 2015.

Edwards, Anne. *Judy Garland: A Biography*. Lanham, MD: Taylor, 2013.

Engle, John. *Surfing in the Movies: A Critical History*. Jefferson, NC: McFarland, 2015.

Eyman, Scott. *Lion of Hollywood: The Life and Legend of Louis B. Mayer*. New York: Simon & Schuster, 2005.

Gado, Frank. *The Passion of Ingmar Bergman*. Durham, NC: Duke University Press, 1986.

Grant, Barry Keith, ed. *American Cinema of the 1960s: Themes and Variations*. New Brunswick, NJ: Rutgers University Press, 2008.

Gray, Beverly. *Seduced by Mrs. Robinson: How* The Graduate *Became the Touchstone of a Generation.* Chapel Hill, NC: Algonquin Books, 2017.

Green, Stanley. *The World of Musical Comedy: The Story of the American Musical Stage as Told Through the Careers of Its Foremost Composers and Lyricists*. South Brunswick, NJ: A.S. Barnes, 1974.

Grobel, Lawrence. *The Hustons: The Life and Times of a Hollywood Dynasty*. New York: Skyhorse, 2014.

Harris, Mark. *Pictures at a Revolution: Five Movies and the Birth of the New Hollywood*. New York: Penguin Books, 2014.

Haskell, Molly. *Steven Spielberg: A Life in Films*. New Haven, CT: Yale University Press, 2017.

Hediger, Ryan. "*Breaking Away* and Vital Materialism: Embodying Dreams of Social Mobility via the Bicycle Assemblage." In *Culture on Two Wheels: The Bicycle in Literature and Film*, edited by Jeremy Withers and Daniel P. Shea, 263–280. Lincoln: University of Nebraska Press, 2016.

Higham, Charles. *Kate: The Life of Katharine Hepburn*. New York: W.W. Norton & Co., 1975.

Hoberman, J. "*Nashville* Contra *Jaws*: Or, 'The Imagination of Disaster' Revisited." In *The Last Great American Picture Show: New Hollywood Cinema in the 1970s*, edited by Thomas Elsaesser, Alexander Horwath, and Noel King, 158–180. Amsterdam: Amsterdam University Press, 2004.

Ingersoll, Earl G. *Filming Forster: The Challenges of Adapting E. M. Forster's Novels for the Screen*. Madison, NJ: Fairleigh Dickinson University Press, 2014.

Kael, Pauline. *For Keeps: 30 Years at the Movies*. New York: Plume, 1994.

Kashner, Sam, and Jennifer MacNair. *The Bad & the Beautiful: Hollywood in the Fifties.* Old Saybrook, CT: Konecky & Konecky, 2002.

Knowlton, Christopher. *Bubble in the Sun: The Florida Boom of the 1920s and How It Brought on the Great Depression*. New York: Simon & Schuster, 2020.

Kornhaber, Donna. *Wes Anderson*. Urbana: University of Illinois Press, 2017.

Leaming, Barbara. *Marilyn Monroe*. New York: Three Rivers Press, 1998.

Lincoln, Sian, and Yannis Tzioumakis, eds. *The Time of Our Lives:* Dirty Dancing *and Popular Culture*. Detroit: Wayne State University Press, 2013.

Long, Robert Emmet. *James Ivory in Conversation: How Merchant Ivory Makes Its Movies*. Berkeley: University of California Press, 2005.

Macnab, Geoffrey. *Ingmar Bergman: The Life and Films of the Last Great European Director.* New York: Palgrave Macmillan, 2009.

Madsen, Axel. *Billy Wilder.* Bloomington: Indiana University Press, 1968.

Massood, Paula J. *Black City Cinema: African American Urban Experiences in Film.* Philadelphia: Temple University Press, 2003.

McGilligan, Patrick. *Alfred Hitchcock: A Life in Darkness and Light.* New York: ReganBooks, 2003.

McIver, Stuart B. *Dreamers, Schemers and Scalawags: The Florida Chronicles.* Sarasota, FL: Pineapple Press, 1994.

Monaco, Paul. *The Sixties: 1960–1969.* New York: Scribner, 2001.

Nashawaty, Chris. Caddyshack*: The Making of a Hollywood Cinderella Story and the Remaking of American Comedy.* New York: Flatiron Books, 2018.

Phillips, Brent. *Charles Walters: The Director Who Made Hollywood Dance.* Lexington: University Press of Kentucky, 2014.

Phillips, Gene D. *Gangsters and G-Men on Screen: Crime Cinema Then and Now.* Lanham, MD: Rowman & Littlefield, 2014.

Seamon, John. *Memory and Movies: What Films Can Teach Us About Memory.* Cambridge: MIT Press, 2015.

Shandley, Robert R. *Runaway Romances: Hollywood's Postwar Tour of Europe.* Philadelphia: Temple University Press, 2009.

Shary, Timothy. *Teen Movies: American Youth on Screen.* New York: Wallflower, 2005.

Sikov, Ed. *On Sunset Boulevard: The Life and Times of Billy Wilder.* New York: Hyperion, 1998.

Silverman, Stephen M. *The Amusement Park: 900 Years of Thrills and Spills, and the Dreamers and Schemers Who Built Them.* New York: Black Dog & Leventhal, 2019.

Spoto, Donald. *The Dark Side of Genius: The Life of Alfred Hitchcock.* New York: Little, Brown & Co.: 1983.

Sullivan, Robert. *Cross Country: Fifteen Years and Ninety Thousand Miles on the Roads and Interstates of America with Lewis and Clark, a Lot of Bad Motels, a Moving Van, Emily Post, Jack Kerouac, My Wife, My Mother-in-Law, Two Kids, and Enough Coffee to Kill an Elephant.* New York: Bloomsbury, 2006.

Sweet, Rosemary. *Cities and the Grand Tour: The British in Italy, c. 1690–1820.* Cambridge, UK: Cambridge University Press, 2015.

Townsley, Michael K. *Steve Hannagan: Prince of the Press Agents and Titan of Modern Public Relations.* Indianapolis: Dog Ear Publishing, 2018.

Vieira, Mark A. *Into the Dark*: The Hidden World of Film Noir, 1941–1950*. Philadelphia: Running Press, 2016.

Whitehead, J.W. *Appraising* The Graduate*: The Mike Nichols Classic and Its Impact in Hollywood.* Jefferson, NC: McFarland, 2011.

Whitney, Allison. "Gidget Goes Hysterical." In *Sugar, Spice, and Everything Nice: Cinemas of Girlhood*, edited by Frances K. Gateward and Murray Pomerance, 55–72. Detroit: Wayne State University Press, 2002.

Zambenedetti, Alberto. *World Film Locations: Florence.* Bristol, UK: Intellect Books, 2014.

JOURNALS AND PERIODICALS

Baltimore Sun

Believer

Cineaste

Condé Nast Traveler

Elle Decor

Entertainment Weekly

Eugene Weekly

Feminist Media Studies

Film & History

Film Comment

Film Quarterly

Hollywood Reporter

International Journal of Historical Archaeology

Jezebel

Life

Los Angeles Times

Mental Floss

New York

New York Times

People

Saturday Evening Post

Screen Education

Surfer

Time

Variety

ONLINE RESOURCES

AAGPBL Players Association (aagpbl.org)

The Age (theage.com.au)

American Film Institute (afi.com)

AMPAS (oscars.org)

BAFTA (bafta.org)

Bruce Brown Films (brucebrownfilms.com)

The Criterion Collection (criterion.com)

The Cut (thecut.com)

D23: The Official Disney Fan Club (d23.com)

Den of Geek (denofgeek.com)

ESPN (espn.com)

HuffPost (huffpost.com)

IMDb (imdb.com)

Indiana University (iu.edu)

Iowa State Fair (iowastatefair.org)

Jonathan Rosenbaum (jonathanrosenbaum.net)

Kansas Historical Society (kshs.org)

National Film Registry (loc.gov)

NPR (npr.org)

Roger Ebert (rogerebert.com)

Swedish Institute (sweden.se)

Tablet Magazine (tabletmag.com)

Turner Classic Movies (tcm.com)

INDEX

ACKNOWLEDGMENTS

Thanks must first go to my most important proofreaders. Eli Arnold is my daily and life-long support and provided a critical mix of encouragement, accountability, research assistance, and coffee. Sharon Thackston is my fellow movie geek, best friend, advisor, thesaurus, film encyclopedia, and sounding board. And to Madison, who sat with me through all of these movies even though she didn't understand them.

This book would have been impossible if not for the love and support of my family, who (among other things) allowed me to have a series of carefree summers. Here's to many more family vacations!

It is a joy to be a part of Turner Classic Movies, which was instrumental in exposing me to films in the first place. Thanks especially to Heather Margolis for her unending support, kindness, and high standards. To Genevieve McGillicuddy for her guidance and our shared love of movies. To General Manager Pola Changnon for her leadership, to the Enterprises team, and to the rest of the TCM staff. And also to former colleagues Shannon Clute, Stina Chyn, and Jennifer

Dorian, who each helped pave a path for me. Thanks as well to Eileen Flanagan, John Renaud, Wendy Gardner, and Jacqulyn Nestinger. And to Aaron Spiegeland at Parham Santana, a partner in crime.

Thanks of course to the wonderful team at Running Press, especially my editor Cindy Sipala for her immediate belief in me, and for her patience and direction along the way. And to designer Jenna McBride, publisher Kristen Kiser, production manager Katie Manning, publicist Seta Zink, and marketing manager Amy Cianfrone.

Jeremy Arnold is both a good friend and an inspiration, providing the model for *Summer Movies* with the form and terrific writing of his own books. Several important people from my academic career also deserve a mention, including professors Matthew Bernstein, Michele Schreiber, and Eddy Von Mueller from Emory University; R. Barton Palmer from Oglethorpe University; and my fellow grad students.

I came to love film because of several influential voices, among them Roger Ebert, Leonard Maltin, and Robert Osborne. They were my early guides to the world of movies; mentors all, though they didn't know it.

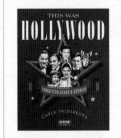

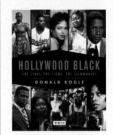

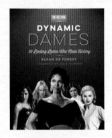

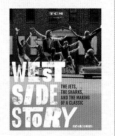
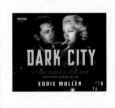

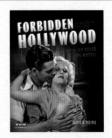